Better Together

harnessing the power of teamwork

Stephen R. Tourville, D.Min.
with Jason A. Tourville, M.A.

Cover design by David Mayne.

<u>DEDICATION</u>

"To the teams and team leaders who may feel their task is too overwhelming. May you discover that being "Better Together" opens the potential of the whole being greater than the sum of your parts!"

ACKNOWLEDGMENTS

Each of our lives is dependent upon many other's influence for us to live a life well lived. Likewise, any book that is worthwhile is generated by more than just the author. My staff and team have not only been the recipients of my experiments in team leadership, they has also been contributors to my thoughts and practical applications of team ministry.

A special thanks to my dear wife, Marjie, who has been my greatest fan since the day we said, "I do!" In addition, my son, Jason A. Tourville, has been a prime mover in motivating and encouraging this volume. It would not exist without him. What an amazing gift he has been to me from my heavenly Father!

<u>WHAT OTHERS ARE SAYING</u>

Steve and Jason Tourville demonstrate in their own ministries the power of teamwork. God does not intend anyone to be a Lone Ranger in ministry. This book will help you either built a team, better the team you're on, or become a better team member yourself!

Dr. George O. Wood
General Superintendent of the Assemblies of God

I find this book to be most timely. We live in an individualistic world where driven individuals are lauded for their "Gold Medal" achievements. Most of us who are called to serve God are not "Gold Medal Winners" but servants of Jesus who want to preach the Gospel, run our race and do our best for our Master. I have found that we are at our most effective when we learn to flow together as a Team with all our Gifts and Calling joining together as one, for the Spirit of God to flow through. There is power in togetherness and power in unity! I believe that this book will be a great help and encouragement to many!

Christopher Alam
World Evangelist; Dynamis World Ministries

Fewer skills are more relevant to today's spiritual leader than the ability to do ministry *through* people and not just *to* them. I am especially compelled by the hands-on learning experiences of ministry practitioners who become great team builders. Their credibility is baked into the product. That is why I so highly recommend this book, Better Together, and the leadership of my friend, Stephen Tourville.

Dr. James Bradford
General Secretary of the Assemblies of God

"Better Together" is more than a catchphrase; it is the motivating story of a self-confessed "average guy" who learned how to harness teamwork to accomplish astounding goals. The valuable lessons learned along the way are the centerpiece and deep reflection is given through the lenses of both the Word of God and human nature. This is a must-have resource for leaders and lay people who want to accomplish God-sized goals...together!

Tim Enloe
Author/Conference Speaker; Holy Spirit Conferences

No one has better modeled the leadership principle that "we are better together" than Dr. Stephen Tourville. Now in his new book, readers will be able to learn the essential tools and the benefits of the idea of leading better together. This book is must-read for anyone seeking to enhance their leadership effectiveness.

Bryan Koch
Lead Pastor GT Church

I absolutely love the them and challenge of this book. Pastors Stephen and Jason have done an amazing job of capturing and modeling this collaborative permission-giving model of ministry. You will be better for reading this and as the title says, be able to do ministry "better together."

Jeff Leake
Lead Pastor at Allison Park Church

CONTENTS

INTRODUCTION: My Story 1

PART #1: The Shaping of a Team Leader

Chapter 1: Early Lesson in Teamwork 9

Chapter 2: Unflappable 17

PART #2: The Formation of a Team

Chapter 3: Hat #1 – The Recruiting Hat 27

Chapter 4: Hat #2 – The Training Hat 41

Chapter 5: Hat #3 – The Coaching Hat 49

PART #3: The Function of a Team

Chapter 6: Teamwork and Emotional Intelligence ... 59

Chapter 7: Teamwork and Cultural Change 73

PART #4: The Fulfillment of a Team

Chapter 8: The Challenges of a Team 87

Chapter 9: The Body of Teamwork 99

Chapter 10: The Trust Equation 109

Additional Resources 123

About the Authors 124

Introduction

MY STORY

"But God how ironic that the longer and better I lead, the more I depend on the skills and expertise of others." Richard Kriegbaum in Leadership Prayers

My spiritual journey began at a young age. At 6 years old I came to understand the importance of receiving Jesus into my heart. As I grew, my view became one of following Jesus as a disciple. Later, learning cognitively became the priority. Reading, study and memorizing Bible verses became critical to me in order to grow in my walk with the Lord.

Going into ministry positions, the tasks associated with my role took center stage. Learning to play the guitar was of personal interest with the added benefit of leading others into God's presence through worship in song. Study of such topics as hermeneutics, homiletics and apologetics added to my needed skills for ministry to others. Eventually, I began to grasp the importance of gaining administrative abilities, which for most of us called to pastoral ministry seems more like a necessary evil than a desired field of study. I came to understand the importance of staying out of God's way so

He could do what He wants to do. I came to realize that He is more concerned about what He is doing in me than what He is doing through me. The final piece for me was realizing the kingdom multiplication effect of what can be accomplished if we don't care who gets the credit and how much God wants to work through His people not just "the leader." The old saying is: "It is better to get ten men to do the work than to do the work of ten men." Our entire network is the team God is using to reach lost people, and we do it *better together*.

"Better Together" has become the phrase in our network that identifies who we are and how we do ministry. It is not used to manipulate our team members to fulfill the goals of the organization as would occur in a hierarchical structure, but it resonates with us because of our commitment to the commission of our Lord Jesus and our commitment to each other in our network. The phrase came out of our brainstorming session while we, as a network staff, were struggling with an appropriate expression that would be true to our ministry culture, the principles of God's Word, and our desire to be fully Pentecostal and evangelical. Unity has always been a critical value among the people of God. The two scriptures that continually resonate in my heart are:

> How good and pleasant it is when God's people live together in unity! It is like precious oil poured on the head, running down on the beard, running down on Aaron's beard, down on the collar of his robe. It is as if the dew of Hermon were falling on Mount Zion. For there the LORD bestows his blessing, even life forevermore. (Psalm 133:1-3)

When the day of Pentecost came, they were all together in one place. Suddenly a sound like the blowing of a violent wind came from heaven and filled the whole house where they were sitting. (Acts 2:1-2)

The value of unity among God's people and especially among those who serve together has obvious practical implications. If team members are pulling in different directions, progress will be impossible. Spiritually, the Lord bestowing His blessing hinges largely on our living together in unity. Receiving "life forevermore" flows naturally from a group of committed followers of Jesus who walk in unity.

I consider myself to be a student of two primary things, the Word of God and human nature. The commitment to Scripture should be a given for any church and her leadership; however, American cultural Christianity is slipping away from centrality and inerrancy of Scripture. If the church and its people are not learning the Word of God, then they are not getting to know God. Doing church biblically does not mean we are unaware of the cultural changes around us. It does mean the Word of God is our "infallible, authoritative rule of faith and conduct (2 Timothy 3:15-17; 1 Thessalonians 2:13; 2 Peter 1:21)[1].

It should be understood the authority of the minister is not derived from the individual's outgoing personality or superior intellect. It comes from the Author of Scripture. Being true to that Source is paramount for effective, long-term eternal results. When we discuss and plan for events and work on our strategies, our team intentionally ponders the biblical truths that drive our decisions. Speakers are chosen with care because of their sound doctrine and what value they can add to our ministers not just their popularity.

---

[1] General Council Statement of Fundamental Truths

Events are planned to give proper priority to the Word of God proclaimed so that our people can be equipped for their responsibilities in serving the Lord.

Human nature is the context for ministry which becomes the variable in how to serve in the world today. Technology, styles, means of communication and graphic designs are constantly morphing. One size no longer fits all. We live in a world of many choices from preferences of cereal for breakfast in the morning to the type of car, and the music we enjoy. The Internet has expanded the options for everyone so that our world is wide open to anyone who chooses to research the possibilities. Anyone can become an expert on anything if they choose. The impact this brings to the way people think and act cannot be overstated. It is true that human nature has not changed much since the beginning of time, but how we function has changed radically. People of my generation have been called aliens in today's culture, and I can tell you from personal experience the truth of that. While I am comfortable with Skype, FaceTime, Facebook and text messaging, I don't get Twitter or Instagram. My grandchildren are comfortable with online shopping, eBooks and all the electronic devices that continue to change the way people interact. I have to work to keep up with these changes. They just seem to flow with it all.

We are naïve if we assume these changes have no bearing on how people in our culture go about their lives and how that influences their view of doing church. Leaders who ignore human nature and cultural and technological changes will not have many opportunities to share Jesus in a relevant, authentic way in a secular society.

One of my cousins has worked the farm for many years. Technology has allowed him to radically gain in efficiency and productivity. This is certainly beyond my expertise, but as I understand it, there are systems that track the birth size of calves produced by a bull so that fathering a calf can be matched with a heifer or cow that can produce the healthy offspring. In a previous generation, the ranches had much fewer options in developing the herd. Now, little is left to chance. Science has made it possible for the farmers to feed masses of people through greater efficiency and productivity.

A part of the cultural change relates to organizational structure. In previous generations a hierarchical approach was often the most effective leadership methodology. When there is a strong militaristic mentality in the culture at large and leaders are trusted to make the major decisions, a top down approach is very effective and often the most efficient. However, when high profile leaders fail to live up to cultural expectations within the church and in the culture in general, when major corporations are no longer seen as a reliable source of financial security and when individuals can, through the use of social media, make significant contributions to others regardless of the geographical proximity, organizational structures tend to become flat. Basically, that means that more people throughout the organization can make a significant contribution regardless of their position within the structure.

This latter development with the PennDel Ministry Network has taken on great significance. There are so many amazing leaders within our fellowship. Because we are *Better Together,* every leader, regardless of a title, has been encouraged and embraced in fulfilling the call God has placed on their lives. The results of the unity within our fellowship has been, in my opinion, nothing short of miraculous.

In the last ten years we have seen many churches planted, thousands of salvations and baptisms in the Holy Spirit and many strengthened in their walk with God. This is not accomplished because of one person's strategic plan, superior intellect, or outstanding spiritual gifts. It happens because, along with our Presbytery and staff, people like Gary Bellis, Brian Bolt, Dave Crosby, Jr., Steven DeFrain, Steve C. DeFrain, Bill Ellis, Chris Foster, Bryan Koch, Brad Leach, Jeff Leake, Sam Masteller, Daniel McNaughton, Phil Menditto, Rodney Murphy, Curt Seaburg, Gerry Stoltzfoos, Dave Twiss and so many others who have a vision to reach lost people for Christ and are released to exercise their gifts.

The story in this book on harnessing the power of teamwork is not just about me, nor about our staff at the Ministry Center. It incorporates the many individuals who make up the leaders, congregations and individuals God has brought together to impact our world for Christ.

As you read, I pray you will receive a fresh vision of what can happen as a team of godly leaders work together for the common goal of reaching our world for Christ by focusing on the role each plays in their God-given calling, serving together as a team under the anointing, power and presence of the Holy Spirit.

PART I
Personal Formation

Chapter 1
EARLY LESSONS IN TEAMWORK

For by the grace given me I say to every one of you:
Do not think of yourself more highly than you ought,
but rather think of yourself with sober judgment,
in accordance with the faith God has distributed to each
of you.
(Romans 12:3)

The year was 1969. An 18 year old young man from the rolling hills of the Ozarks deep in the heart of Missouri journeyed to his freshman year at Northeast Bible Institute (NBI) in the suburbs of Philadelphia. He was 6-foot, 4-inches tall and all of 175 lbs. As he followed God's call to prepare for vocational ministry as a pastor, two months into his first semester he found himself playing on the basketball team.

The campus was at Green Lane, PA. The gym was hardly fitting for a classroom, none-the-less for a basketball team. The floor was laid with concrete, and the support beams were located where the current day 3-point line occupies. With little actual experience, this team would soon teach him much about future leadership. Past the skinned knees, bruised elbows, and chronic shin-splints from

9

playing on a concrete floor... the lessons between the lines would not be quickly forgotten.

I was that young man, Stephen Robert Tourville. What has become the rallying cry in my recent years of ministry was a simple reality for our inexperience, and over-matched basketball squad of would-be ministers. *We Are Better Together*!

We certainly were not much by ourselves.

I surely needed to learn the lesson of teamwork!

My prior education and experience taught me much of hard work, independence, prayer, reliance upon God, and many disciplines. Of all, education was most valued. Teamwork would have to be something I discovered, but a most valuable discovery indeed. It would not be a lesson learned in a classroom, but one that would begin with the round ball in hand. I would continue to digest the lessons, the skills and the experience of teamwork through the years to come.

It was here that harnessing the power of teamwork began in my life. Later it would overflow to my ministry.

WHY THIS BOOK

I've hesitated writing a book as I've always considered myself to be the average guy. There are those across the Kingdom of God who are obvious 10-talent servants of the Lord. They pastor the mega-churches, lead the great institutions within the Christian world, and impact our culture for the Kingdom. When they preach, you stand in awe at their oratory skills. Their musical ability tames the wild beasts. They motivate and mobilize the masses with their vision casting skills... and some of them are happy to let you know all their accomplishments while many humbly serve with distinction and excellence.

Don't take me wrong, the Kingdom of God needs these 10-talent leaders. I've just never considered myself to be one of them. Interestingly enough, that became the motivating reason behind this book. The majority of those who Christ saves, redeems and calls into Kingdom ministry (whether in full-time work, or as lay-leaders) are... what shall I call us... AVERAGE!

I know, it sounds like a 4-letter word. We are told to be extraordinary, be a giant slayer, believe for the best, have faith for the grand vision, etc... In reality I truly believe we can be all these things, and yet still be AVERAGE! (Ooo, I hate that word)

Average really isn't that bad. Throughout Scripture, God used the "average" to reveal Himself. Recently Matt Keller in his book *God of the Underdogs*[2], lists examples of how God used the average (underdog). He writes, "*Every person God chose to use in a great way in the Bible was an underdog. Every person God used had a justifiable excuse for why he or she couldn't or shouldn't be used by God to accomplish great things.*"

For the 1% of top leaders, sorry this book is not for you. For the rest of us who simply want to offer our loaves and fishes into the hands of the Lord so he can break and multiply as He sees fit... This book is for YOU! This book is for the underdogs. This book is for the AVERAGE!

NO SUCH THING AS THE PERFECT TEAM

Needless to say, our Bible school basketball team played with much passion and heart, but we often found ourselves out skilled and outsized. I'm not even sure we

---

[2] God of the Underdogs: When the odds are against you, God is for you. Nashville, TN. Nelson Books, 2013. (p.xvii)

could have been called average. It was a good reminder that none of us were called to the NBA, but to Christ's church. These college years taught me that a team needed to depend on each other. To this day, some of my closest friends and colleagues are from the early years at NBI.

This would also explain why my favorite team during the 80's was the Boston Celtics. Although many of the players would become famous, they were not much to look at by themselves. The great Larry Bird was never faster, stronger, nor could he jump higher than his counterparts, but he would consistently dominate each game he played. Kevin McHale somehow always got the job done. The chief, Robert Parish, would get those ugly-high arching shots to fall. He had to, because I'm not sure he ever elevated off the ground.

I could list each player and similar accounts would arise. However, the point I would like to make is that together they were amazing. They figured out a way to be **better together**!

The real job of leaders (coaches, CEO's, pastors, and foremen)…is getting the most from your team.

Over the following decades I would pastor four churches in a variety of settings and cultures across the state of Pennsylvania. The majority of these churches would now be termed "turn-around churches." However, we had yet to develop the different labels to stamp each kingdom expression. From our first role in Knoxville, PA where I learned early lessons of developing a schedule for sermon preparation, prayer time, administrative tasks, and visitation... to the suburbs of Philadelphia, I quickly learned that pastoring was less about ME and more about the WE!

However, the WE was not always as united as I thought it should be, and certainly not as united as my college buddies and I had been. I learned that if I couldn't get the team moving together, WE COULDN'T MOVE FORWARD. This is especially true in the church when there are significant differences in doctrinal points of view. The challenge of the extreme faith movement (positive confession) created discord in many congregations, ours included. The focus of some in the church was so much on healing and positive confession that community impact and outreach were considered less important. As painful as it was for these individuals to leave our church, it was necessary for that to happen if we were to move forward together in unity. Once the congregation was again united, we began to experience the forward movement for which we were aiming.

Aside... by saying "get the team moving together" it certainly doesn't mean that everyone always got on board and made life easy (specifically my life). We did, however, figure out a way to move forward! Forward movement is the #1 result of what it means to be **better together**.

Many of the bumps and bruises I've endured through the years in bringing people together, developing teams and assuring that the sum of the parts are greater than the parts themselves are recorded in this book. However, I must warn you, becoming Better Together doesn't happen on its own. In fact I truly believe the 2nd law of physics even applies to leadership, "*every system left to its own devices always tends to move from order to disorder[3].*"

The reason there is NEVER a one-size-fits-all approach to leadership is because it is the art of bringing order from disorder... harnessing the power of teamwork is constantly dealing in chaos. Unfortunately, too many times we get lost in the chaos ourselves. It is a leader's role

---

[3] http://www.talkorigins.org/faqs/thermo/probability.html

(whether in a church, a sports team, a business or a family) to move the state of "things" from disorder to order. The only way we're Better Together is if men and women rise to the challenge, put the WE before the ME, and begin to harness the power of the team.

Anyone who has followed a great leader can understand my personal sense of being over my head when I was elected to lead the Pennsylvania-Delaware District of the Assemblies of God. Rev. Philip Bongiorno, affectionately known as "Bro. B" to most of us in our fellowship, led the district for 24 years. He accomplished many high watermarks including growth in the number of churches, adherents, the purchase and development of the Conference Center, and founding Heritage Investment Services (HIS Fund). His generation achieved great things through the General Council of the Assemblies of God. People such as Charles Crank and Alman Bartholomew, etc. brought the fellowship to a higher level. As a new superintendent, how do you top that? Where do you go from there? I was confident in my call and God's direction so I knew who I was and what was needed.

If you are in any type of leadership position in your community, job or church, being a team-builder is what God has called you to be and to do. The greatest team ever established was done so by God. We call it the church. None can doubt that this "team" has become a formidable force across the globe.

THE BUTTERFLY EFFECT

The pages of this book will help you connect the dots of what it takes to allow God to maximize His gifts in you, your team and perhaps even those outside your team. While some may focus on leadership, others focus on disciplines (spiritual, physical, mental), others focus on organizational systems, and still others on chance or divine providence, I've discovered that each area of discipline affects the other. No aspect of our life, team, or leadership is isolated from each other. They are all connected.

In what is called the chaos theory, the **butterfly effect** is the **sensitive dependence on initial conditions** in which a small change in one state of a deterministic nonlinear system can result in large differences in a later state. Sorry, my inner geek just came out.

The butterfly effect describes how everything effects everything. Andy Andrews wrote in his web blog about the 1963 doctoral research of Edward Lorenz. He says, "In it, he theorized that a butterfly might flap its wings, moving molecules of air into motion that in turn moved other molecules of air, eventually becoming able to shift weather patterns on the other side of the world. Of course, in 1963, the theory was ridiculous. And the New York Academy of Science said so[4]." However, the truth is that teamwork is like the butterfly effect. Each area of our lives, ministry, and business effect the other.

What I will describe in the chapters that follow is what it truly takes to harness the power of teamwork. I must warn you, at face value, the principles and values may not be what you first think of when considering teamwork. But as you'll see, teamwork is the result of the right relationships, the right decisions, right living and the right movement. It is a leaders role to move the state of "things" from disorder to order.

So all you AVERAGE people, buckle up and let's enjoy this ride. The only way we are *Better Together* is if

---

[4] Andrews, Andy. "The Butterfly Effect." Web blog post. Andy Andrews. 18, Nov. 2009. Web. 5 Feb. 2016.
http://www.andyandrews.com/the-butterfly-effect/

both men and women rise to the challenge, put the WE before the ME, and begin to harness the power of the team.

Chapter 2
UNFLAPPABLE

Better a patient person than a warrior,
one with self-control than one who takes a city.

(Proverbs 16:32)

MISS AMERICA

My daughter and wife were cuddled up on the couch. The excitement of my youngest was palpable as she was allowed to stay up later than normal. My son and I were driven from their presence. Although not from the women's doing, we were simply uninterested in the Miss America Pageant.

It has been their custom for decades to watch, score, and vote for who they think should be the next Miss America. Even today with 1000 miles separating them, they will call each other on the phone, with my daughter-in-law texting periodically, all trying to guess. It is an estrogen filled event.

Over 50 young ladies compete in this event each year. It is a whirlwind of interviews, hair dos, make-up sessions, jewelry coordination, and of course wardrobe changes. As I have caught bits and pieces of these pageants through the years (ok, you caught me, I have watched some of them too.

Please don't make me turn in my man-card), I have been impressed that these otherwise high-maintenance women are able to change wardrobes so quickly.

For all you men out there that wait patiently for your woman take 2 hours to get ready for 1 night out, I suggest you encourage them to watch the Miss American Pageant. On second thought, perhaps you'd best hold your peace, wait patiently and let them know how beautiful they are when they finally appear! Seriously, hold any other comments to yourself.

After 30+ years of full-time pastoral ministry, I found myself in a series of transitions that eventually landed me in the role of District Superintendent for our fellowship. My role would come to oversee 400+ churches and about 1200 ministers in the Pennsylvania-Delaware region. It addition to this I would also be involved in the national level of leadership.

While I was relatively confident in the role of pastoring and what was expected of me, I quickly found out that my new ministry "assignment" would require something much more. I actually felt like one of those contestants from the Miss America Pageant constantly changing my leadership outfits according to what was required, often many times in the same meeting.

My late friend, Paul Grabill, served with me for many years. He knew me as a pastor, a district official, district staff person, at the National office, and finally when I took my role as our District Superintendent (our Fellowship's Regional Director of PA & DE). Paul knew our region as well as anyone and was as passionate a leader as any I've worked with. He liked to stir the pot, probe deeper, and always was a bundle of energy.

A couple of years into my role, Paul and I were

traveling together from one of our many meetings. Much of what we were doing was creating new structures through relationship. I knew in my spirit that the vision we were discovering could not be a top-down proclamation. Not only did we need the grass roots to be involved (*a come to our party and participate approach*), but we needed it to be the ground-swell of those on the front lines pushing it.

My role in the early stages of this process used all the listening skills I had developed through the decades. I listened to needs, frustrations, ideas, reasons why change couldn't happen, reasons why change had to happen. It was from these, sometime frustrating meeting, that we developed what now is called our C^3 approach to ministry (Catalyst, Connect, Coaching).

It was as we traveled to one of these meetings when Paul looked over at me and said, "Pastor Steve, you know what you are?" I really wasn't sure what was coming next, so I just waited. He continued, "I've watched and sat through many meetings and committees now. I've come to a conclusion about you. You're..." He paused in thought for a moment as he always chose his words carefully. "You're UNFLAPPABLE!"

I laughed awkwardly out loud not fully knowing exactly what he meant and then responded, "Thanks Paul, I'll take that as compliment." "Good," was his only response. A moment or two passed and we were off in conversation down another rabbit trail.

As I've had time to ponder his description of me, I've come to embrace it. He wasn't describing me as stubborn or uncaring. He just knew that no matter the weather, the mood in the meeting, the resistance or support we encountered, I remained unmoved... unflappable. I didn't have to stand up and make the proclamation from atop the mountain... "This is the way we're going... either you're for us or you're against us." Neither would I cower in a corner waiting for someone else to ask the hard questions or refocus the group.

I truly believe that being UNFLAPPABLE has allowed the strongest and best leaders of our network to shine, grow, expand and contribute in their own way. Being UNFLAPPABLE is never threatened from a position of insecurity and never dominates from a position of power. It is being secure in the Lord and in yourself!

Being UNFLAPPABLE provides the emotional consistency for team members to both follow and trust. Without this quality, every breeze of disappointment and thrill of victory destabilizes a team. I told my son as he was entering pastoral ministry, "Don't let you highs be too high, or your lows be too low."

In August of 2011, Paul lost his battle with cancer, but won the battle of life as he joined the Church triumphant. I will never forget his words concerning the potential death of any believer. He would say, "well, you can't scare a Christian with heaven." I miss my friend as I try to remain UNFLAPPABLE in the midst of changes and challenges.

The title of this book, *Better Together*, was not just a catch-phrase meant to unify our churches and value different opinions. It is a theological conviction I've held from Ephesians 4:16, "From him *(Jesus)* the whole body, joined and held together by every supporting ligament, *grows and builds itself up* in love, as each part does its work." If our network of hundreds of churches was going to reach its full potential, I knew I couldn't *grow and build* it myself. Each member of the body, each pastor, local congregation, deacons, etc... had to do their part as well.

This isn't always the quickest way or easiest, but it is the healthiest. I agree with the great civil rights leader, Martin Luther King, Jr. who said, "A genuine leader is not a searcher for consensus but a molder of consensus." Harnessing the power of teams molds consensus, leads the group toward an uncertain tomorrow, and keeps everyone focused on the mission and goals.

Anyone who works with and through teams understands how difficult consensus can be. Everyone has their own needs, expectations, fears, and agendas. If you think opinionated church members are challenging, try doing it with a bunch of high capacity, gifted pastors. But building consensus doesn't have to be done in such a way that it leaves a wake of blood shed as you pass. Neither do you abdicate your leadership role.

Unflappable may be an unconventional term, but it summarizes some qualities that are critical to your effectiveness as a team leader. Emotional Intelligence studies have demonstrated that effective leadership requires more than a high intelligence quotient (IQ) to lead with excellence. As important as it is to have an intellectual grasp of the realities the team faces, the personal and social competencies of a leader exert great influence on the team. Here are some questions you might want to ask yourself with regard to how your team members feel about you as their leader.

1. **Do my team members feel safe with me as their leader?**

    By this I am not suggesting you and your team should never take any risk in order for them to feel safe. Their sense of safety or security with you as their lead relates to the confidence they have in your character and your predictability in the face of challenges. Pastor Bill (not his real name) became so agitated with one of his board members that one night after service the two of them met in the church parking lot with angry words being exchanged and they came very close to a physical altercation, a nice way to say "a fight." The pastor lost all credibility with the people. No apology would ever erase the image the people had of their pastor losing his temper. He was no longer a safe leader.

2. **Do they see me as consistent?**

Just as children need their parents to be as good as their word and to have their actions to be consistent with their words, so our team members need for our words and actions to align. To make a promise and not keep that promise demonstrates an inconsistency that is unacceptable. That, in turn, must be demonstrated over an extended period of time. No one has a perfect record on this, and people will forgive our failures, but there is a limit that, if exceeded, will undermine your credibility with them.

3. **Am I trustworthy and worthy of their respect?**

The Scripture tells us to "abstain from all appearance of evil" (I Thess. 5:22). In essence, avoiding evil is not sufficient. In addition, even its appearance should be avoided. Why? Because our testimony for Christ is very important as we represent Him. Those on your team will also look at your actions and evaluate them, not based on your motives or intentions but from their point of view. As the pastor of a local church for many years, I never allowed my name to be a signature for signing the church checks. It was my way of avoiding the potential of any accusation of impropriety in our church finances. It was critical that I conduct our financial affairs in a way that provided accountability and openness because I knew if I lost their respect, I could no longer lead them.

This next section will begin to give you a few hooks to hang your coat on. While you can't make things happen on your own, there are certainly many ways leaders short circuit the potential of their church, organization and teams. Hopefully, you will learn a bit more about your specific role as team leader.

Depending on the answers to these questions, contemplate, then develop a strategy in answering the same questions in the following manner.

1. What steps can I take so my team feels safe with me as their leader?

_____

_____

_____

2. Have I been inconsistent, and if so, how do I change so I will be a consistent leader of my team?

_____

_____

_____

3. What steps can I take to earn my team's respect and be more trustworthy?

_____

_____

_____

A guiding principle of ministry is to never do ministry alone. We are all strengthened by surrounding ourselves with mentors and coaches that will help us grow in our skills and capacities as leaders. "As iron sharpens iron, so one man sharpens another." (Proverbs 27:17)

PART II
THE
FORMATION
OF A TEAM
The Hats of a Team Leader

Chapter 3

HAT #1

THE RECRUITING HAT

Two are better than one, because they
have a good return for their labor.
(Ecclesiastes 4:9)

LEARNING YOUR ROLE

Teams and teamwork don't form or occur on their own, at least not good teams. What does happen all by themselves are mobs. Whether in the capital in Egypt, to the streets of Los Angeles, mobs are capable of forming and mobilizing without much coordination, planning or strategy.

Teams on the other hand have to be built, dare I say "crafted." Winning teams take this very seriously. Every collegiate and professional team understands the need and tries their best to build a championship team. The temptation exists for the leader to be surrounded by people of similar disposition and giftings. However, the adage is true, individuals should focus on their strengths while

27

organizations should strengthen their weaknesses. Developing a championship team requires team members that will supplement each other so that the whole will be stronger than the sum of the parts. There are at least three hats every leader must wear in order to build a winning team. In this chapter we are discussing the recruiting hat.

RECRUITING HAT

The first hat is the simplest concept to grasp, but the hardest to implement. The smaller the organization, church or school, the more difficult it is to recruit. Without much to offer, it is difficult to recruit the talent necessary to go to the next level.

Of course having talent doesn't solve all an organizations problems. Once talent is obtained, it must also be managed and allocated.

Three concepts are critical in the recruiting process. The first revolves around the question, Should I hire for character or skill?" Obviously, there may be a certain level of skills that are required for specific positions. Hiring a secretary without typing skills or computer literacy would be silly. However, bringing on someone with extraordinary speed of typing who is a liar and thief is also absurd. My suggestion is to think in terms of hiring for character and training for skills as long as the individual has the fundamental potential to be trained in those skills.

Second, discover the individual's personal passion before bringing them onto your team. If they are passionate about what you ask them to do, there will be no need for you to micromanage their efforts. If they are not passionate about their responsibilities, there is no leader that can keep them motivated. The internal drive of the individual, not the financial remuneration, drives that person toward excellence.

Third, it is very important to surround yourself with leaders who are different from you in both spiritual gifts and temperament. Quite frankly, it is sometimes easier to get along with people who think the same way we do, but if you can discern your personal strength and weakness, then you can surround yourself with others who will compliment you by shoring up your areas of weakness. Since you need to focus on your strengths if you are to fulfill your greatest potential, you probably don't need others like yourself. Find people of character, skills and passion who will partner with you as a team member and together make a difference in our world.

For those who work in the church world as I have, your team will make or break you. This is true if you are the lead pastor, staff pastor, department leader or ministry leader. As responsibilities increase, so does the reality of this principle. A leader must wear the recruiting hat.

A church planter's earliest job and continuous job becomes that of recruiting their team. Often the most successful are those who are able to build the best team early in the process. The recruiting hat involves two groups of people. The first group is comprised of the people you inherit. It is a big mistake to assume these individual are already onboard. You must recruit them to accept your methods of leadership. The second group is those who are not yet present. Keep a constant, watchful eye for key individuals.

Those who are leading turnaround churches must also build and recruit their team. A common misconception for these leaders is that they must use those who are already in positions of leadership in the church. While you may need to work with them, a turnaround leader must figure out if they can work through them. The reality is that a leader must sometimes choose who they want to keep on the team and who they must be willing to lose. Bottom line questions: Who do you need on your team and what does your team need?

WHO DO YOU NEED ON YOUR TEAM?

When answering this question, think in terms of actions and attitudes.

First, as you consider your church, ministry, or organization, determine what specific actions, roles and duties you need to fill. There will be roles you need to fill immediately (i.e., children's ministry, music ministry, greeter/connections ministry, etc...) and other roles that would be nice to have, but are roles that could be filled in the near future, but not mission critical (i.e., Small Group ministry)

Who you need will be determined by the current state of the ministry (size & age of the congregation, current ministries and expectations) and will ultimately be determined by your vision for the future. However, in order to lead well in the future (or even have a future), a discerning leader must lead well in the present as well. Work with the current realities you are facing, but never lose vision of the future realities that God has called you to lead toward.

Three questions you may want to spend a few moments answering are:

1. What will be required to move the ministry forward?

_____

_____

2. **Who is currently on the team that can help you move in that direction?**

_____

_____

3. **What is the ideal sequence of adding others to the team to accomplish that direction?**

_____

_____

TEAM ATTITUDE

Critical to the ministry moving forward is to determine who will be on your team. But once you build your team or perhaps your team has been inherited, their actions (or roles) must also be seasoned with the right attitude. John Maxwell has written much about attitude. "Good attitudes among players do not guarantee a team's success, but bad attitudes guarantee its failure." [5]

Guarding the overall attitude that permeates your team is mission critical and must be done immediately, passionately and regularly. Below are a few of the attitudes that will kill the forward movement of the ministry:

1. **COMPLACENCY**
   This attitude says, "We've never done it that way before." Or "We don't do it that way here." Complacency is like an anchor to the soul of the church. It becomes organizational laziness and plows the ruts of ruin.

---

[5] Maxwell, John. The 17 indisputable laws of teamwork. Nashville, TN. Thomas Nelson Publishers, 2001. (p. 106)

2. **OWNERSHIP**

These people say something to the effect of, "This is my area of ministry, don't touch it." It may be phrased quite differently, but the attitude is the same. The reason this attitude is so toxic is that it divides the church into me vs. them (and you're typically the them).

3. **FATALIST**

The fatalistic attitude comments, "No one wants to do anything here." Or asks the question, "Will it really make a difference." If a leader or pastor doesn't guard their heart and mind, this attitude is one of the quickest to creep into our vocabulary. On the contrary, we are called to speak life.

4. **CONTROL**

It may sound differently, but the basic message is, "I'm not following you, I've been here longer and I'm in charge. If you don't like it you can leave." In Gene Wood's book *Leading Turnaround Churches*, he calls this the **98% Principle**[6]. Control boils down to the question, who will lead and who will follow?" In my personal experience, the majority of ministry conflict comes down to control issues. An effective leader must maintain a balance between strong leadership and servant leadership. It is never appropriate to exercise dictatorial authority, but neither is it biblical for the leader to abdicate spiritual authority. The sheep should not lead the shepherd nor the shepherd sheer the sheep.

---

[6] Wood, Gene. Leading turnaround churches. St. Charles: Church Smart Resources, 2001 (p. 47).

WHAT DOES YOUR TEAM NEED?

1. They need a leader who LISTENS

Listening is the art of hearing, feeling & understanding. Those that you lead need to listen to you, but equally important is that YOU NEED TO LISTEN to them. Without good and intentional listening, you become disconnected and irrelevant.

Whether it is parenting or pastoring, listening is critical to your influence. After all, why should someone listen to us if we are not willing to listen to them. I love what Stephen R. Covey writes, "Most people do not listen with the intent to understand; they listen with the intent to reply."*[7] How can we really lead if we don't first understand?

A true leader listen to the needs of those they lead, and they listen to those who benefit from their leadership (customers, community & congregants). To whom are you listening and what has your attention?

There are those who listen to all the complaints, while others listen to all the accolades. Some listen to their fears, others listen to the experts. There are so many voices, but often we listen to the wrong things.

---

[7]Covey, Stephen R., The seven habits of highly effective people. New York: Simon and Schuster, 1989 (p. 239).

Pastors must learn to filter out the unhelpful noises. It is not that we ignore and stop listening, but rather we learn how to become aware.

Being "**aware**" can be defined as having knowledge or perception of a situation or fact. It allows us to have proper viewpoint allowing us to lead ourselves and others. If a leader is not self-aware, they are rarely aware of others. May I add, be very aware of what is called "self talk." We all have these voices in our heads. Being aware of your own thoughts is also listening. Being self-aware helps to discern your own perception that may be healthy or unhealthy. Note the difference and take steps to correct improper thought patterns. "Finally, brothers and sisters, whatever is true, whatever is noble, whatever is right, whatever is pure, whatever is lovely, whatever is admirable—if anything is excellent or praiseworthy—think about such things. Whatever you have learned or received or heard from me, or seen in me—put it into practice. And the God of peace will be with you." Philippians 4:8-9

2. They need a leader who LEADS

When boiled down to its root, leadership is an act of integrity. It says we will do what we say we will do, because what we say is important is truly important, and what is instructed by the Lord must become a reality in our church. Your passionate conviction about this determines your resolute direction and integrity in your leadership.

In each of the churches I pastored there were whose who wanted to be close in relationship with me and my family. Since my motives were pure (at least I thought they were), I assumed others were as well. While this is true most of the time, it is discovered only during times of conflict.

Once such relationship became toxic during the Christmas program. Our "friends" disagreed with our music pastor because they "felt" like they needed a different kind of microphone than the one they were assigned. It became such a source of conflict they brought it to my attention in order to petition for a ruling in their favor. They tried to leverage their relationship with me to get what they wanted. Without going into all the details, I informed them that I trusted the leadership of our music pastor who was organizing the production and trusted the decision he made was best for the overall production as a whole.

By the time the ordeal was over, they left the church and abandoned our relationship. It broke my heart! Every leader, and certainly every pastor, has experienced this type of painful event. But to allow one to dictate, would be to abdicate what I was entrusted (called and hired) to do... LEAD. You need to lead first, and be a friend second!

Leadership assumes there is movement toward a future location, position, goal or vision. While a leader (pastor, CEO, etc...) may not know all the answers to the "how" questions, they must be securely convinced as to the "where" question.

Where are we headed as a team?

_____

_____

_____

3. They need a leader who LOVES

A leader who loves is not comprised of an emotional or a mushy, romantic relationship, but they do have "skin in the game." Perhaps you've heard it said: *people don't care how much you know unless they know how much you care.*

Leaders give more than our time, we give part of ourselves. True leadership is personal! This is the reason we feel so deeply, shed so many tears, get frustrated beyond belief, and why so many pastors deal with depression at some level or the other. A recent article on www.ChurchLeaders.com put it this way,

"Being a pastor—a high-profile, high-stress job with nearly impossible expectations for success—can send one down the road to depression, according to pastoral counselors. "We set the bar so high that most pastors can't achieve that," said H.B. London, vice president for pastoral ministries at Focus on the Family, based in Colorado Springs, Colo. "And because most pastors are people-pleasers, they get frustrated and feel they can't live up to that." When pastors fail to live up to demands imposed by themselves or others they often "turn their frustration back on themselves," leading to self-doubt and to feelings of failure and hopelessness, said Fred Smoot, executive director of Emory Clergy Care in Duluth, Georgia."*[8]

The trouble with our imperfect love is that often we love the wrong things. We allow the wrong things to gain access to our heart. We carry burdens we were never meant to carry. Proverbs 4:23 reminds us, "Above all else, guard your heart, for everything you do flows from it." (NIV)

Don't take me wrong, it is not that we shouldn't feel, just that we should guard our hearts in the process. To help with this there are two specific areas that would be helpful to define so you guard your heart, yet still lead with love. They are compassion & conviction.

What plights, problems and pains cause **compassion** to rise within you?

Areas of Compassion	**Why does this affect you**
_____	_____
_____	_____
_____	_____
_____	_____
_____	_____
_____	_____
_____	_____

---

[8] http://www.churchleaders.com/pastors/pastor-articles/144651-silent-suffering-pastors-and-depression.html

What are non-negotiable characteristics of your leadership that are true **convictions**?

Convictions   **Why is this a non-negotiable**

_____   _____

                                    _____

_____   _____

                                    _____

_____   _____

                                    _____

_____   _____

                                    _____

THE DRAFT

One of the biggest events for sports enthusiasts comes yearly. It is not the Super Bowl, the World Series, or the NBA Championships. It is the DRAFT! There are millions of dollars at stake, dreams are determined, and the fate of many families hang in the balance.

Experts pontificate, predicting what team will draft whom. Sometimes they're right, many times they are wrong. In 1992 the Louisiana State University 7-foot center by the name of Shaquille O'Neal was drafted by the Orlando Magic.

Like the 54 other athletes drafted in the first 2-rounds, when his name was called, he proceeded to the front and was handed a team cap, a jersey, and a handshake from David Stern. The cap is nothing more than a $20 piece of memorabilia, but it provided the draftee with a sense of belonging and identity.

When you recruit your team, you may not give them a cap and a jersey. However, these elements we've covered so far enable you to provide the same sense of belonging and identity to your team. All great leaders provide more than a job or a position. True leaders provide a team!

An additional issue should be addressed at this point. Recruiting team members is a never ending process. In athletic teams someone in the organization must constantly be looking for the next prospect to be recruited to the team. Professional athletic teams tend to recruit from college players, colleges from high schools, and varsity teams from Jr. Varsity teams. The leader who recruits a team of players and assumes that task is done once and for all is either ignorant or naïve.

Every ministry or corporate leader must always be on the lookout for individuals who can be brought into the system in the future. Why is this true?

First, as God blesses your efforts as a team, the opportunity to gain additional influence and expand your horizons means difference skills and talents will be required in order to keep pace with the needs that will surface.

Second, not everyone on your team will continue to buy into the direction God is leading you and the team. The kinds of persons required at one size of organization is different from the kind of persons needed for a larger group. In a church, for example, some believers are comfortable with a church of 100 members, but when God blesses and more people come to Christ, they cannot make the transition to a church of three or four hundred. Unless team members are able to transition their perspective and grow or change their role and expectations, they will not stay long-term.

A leader will need to affirm these members and allow them to find where they are able to serve effectively while at the same time finding additional members for the team who can bring the necessary character and skills for the ministry to continue to move forward.

So while recruiting is an ongoing process, developing the team becomes the next stage for development. Let's discuss that in chapter four.

Chapter 4
HAT #2 - THE TRAINING HAT

The king said to me, "What is it you want?" Then I
prayed to the God of heaven, [5] and I answered the king,
"If it pleases the king and if your servant has found favor
in his sight, let him send me to the city in Judah where my
ancestors are buried so that I can rebuild it."
(Nehemiah 2:4-5)

TRAINING HAT

Once you have recruited and built your team, the next job is to train them. The training or development of a team cannot be delegated. While outsiders can be utilized, in order to harness the power of teamwork, your team must be developed, and you must lead that march.

UCLA iconic coach, John Wooden, understood the need to develop the athletes he recruited to his team. Like all great coaches, he understood the need to develop the person, not just the player.

He was not only developing basketball players but also

41

developing young men. His paradigm developed during Wooden's childhood as he watched his father's farm repossessed. His father, Joshua Wooden, keep a positive attitude, never complaining. It was here Wooden's own definition of success grew, "Success is peace of mind, which is a direct result of self-satisfaction in knowing you made the effort to become the best of which you are capable[9]." Success is what Wooden taught his players. His strategy was holistic in nature. Basketball was only the means to that end.

Holistic development simply means growing in every area of life. It is a balanced approach to a developmental model. *"Real leadership development starts from a much broader place than "career planning." It begins with a holistic vision of one's life, in all its richness. To achieve improved business performance, leaders need to be emotionally engaged in their self-development. And that requires connecting the efforts of what really matters to them.[10]"*

Development of this style goes beyond courses and seminars. It weaves itself into every day conversations, the little details of relationships, and into arenas of life not directly associated with your leadership role in that person's life. I love what Wooden says about his own development, "I attribute my emotional balance, which I feel is critical to playing and coaching success, to my father."

While it is certainly touching to read of his father's role, what I would like you to notice is his comment about "emotional balance." Today we hear much about vision,

---

[9] Williams, Pat. <u>Coach Wooden: The 7 principles that shaped his life and will change your</u>. Grand Rapids: Revel a division of Baker Publishing Group, 2011.

[10] Goleman, Daniel. <u>Primal leadership: Realizing the power of emotional intelligence</u>. Boston: Harvard Business Review Press; 1st edition, 2002. (p. 119).

passion, being missional, etc., but when was the last time "emotional balance" was acknowledged as contributing to someone's success. It is little wonder Coach Wooden holds the NCAA record of collegiate basketball championships.

It is this concept of "emotional balance," or what others have termed in modern terminology as emotional intelligence that harnesses the power of a team. Why? Teamwork is an emotional and messy business, with power struggles, egos, and endless combinations of personalities.

An emotionally intelligent leader builds unity among team members and allows them to break through glass ceilings previously thought to be lids that suppressed their potential.

Perhaps the following questions will help you explore this aspect of development of your team, and even your own life.

1. How would emotional balance strengthen my leadership and team dynamics?

_____

_____

_____

2. What would the development of the emotional balance of my team produce? How might that balance be developed?

_____

_____

_____

3. **In what ways is my emotional balance building walls (isolating potential team members) and in what ways am I building bridges?**

_____

_____

_____

4. **Are there any conversations I have been avoiding but need to occur for the betterment of the team as a whole?**

_____

_____

_____

When I accepted the role as our regional leader, I immediately took inventory of the top-notch leaders in our movement and other fellowships similar to ours. It was amazing to see what God had done through the Pentecostal movement, both in the states and around the world. The Spirit of God had birthed our fellowship as a grass roots movement, not centered on an individual who started the Assemblies of God, but through the efforts and commitment of a wide host of Spirit-filled leaders who were passionate about reaching our world for Christ.

At the district level, the builder generation had established the structures, both organizationally and the facilities that would facilitate the growth and development of the movement. There seemed to be a consistency of that quality of leaders in many parts of the General Council and certainly that was true in Pennsylvania and Delaware. The question I faced was within the context of a changing culture where organizations were becoming flatter rather than having a hierarchy structure. How could we, as a district/region, more effectively structure ourselves for the yet unfulfilled task of reaching our region and world for Christ?

I recognized the potential but was overwhelmed by the challenge. So I did the only thing I knew to do. I did the one thing I had been doing my whole life. Nehemiah gave me marching orders as I read that he prayed to the Lord and spoke to the king. Prayer always sounds like the super-spiritual answer you give before you give the inspiring answer. But for me, I knew I had to pray. Sometimes we are better at talking about prayer than we are at praying. In the various roles I have filled throughout my life, I have always had a sense of dependence on the Lord. I just knew that without God's blessings and anointing, His kingdom work could not be accomplished. Our task in the kingdom of God, and especially as Pentecostals, is not about organizational structures and slick business maneuvers. Except the Lord build the house, we labor in vain.

As I spent time waiting upon the Lord, I was overcome by what He was putting in my heart. I knew it was the Lord depositing these gems in my soul, for I dared not aspire to do more than many of the great leaders I had looked up to. After all, I am just a boy from the Ozarks... remember!

It was in this position of prayer, helplessness, and humility (which always sounds better than it feels) that His still small voice whispered into my ears. He breathed into my spirit the words, "I will give you the people you need, to do what I want you to do!"

TALK TO THE KING

In addition to praying, I've continued the process of study, investigation of options, talking with others and getting counsel from many sources. The practical is part of the process.

We often fall into one of two traps. The first trap is to assume that if we pray, God will do whatever He wants done. Now, I do believe in the sovereignty of God. He rules overall and "works out everything in conformity with the purpose of his will" (Ephesians 1:11). Everything begins and ends with Him.

The second trap is to assume that if we plan, strategize, work hard, and do everything right we will then enjoy success. "If you build it, they will come" expresses a popular view that church leaders often embrace. Certainly, any organization is stronger through vision casting, strategic planning, team building, etc., but the church is to be more than an organization. The church is to be an organism – a living entity whose life is initiated by and sustained through the breath of the Spirit of God.

Avoiding these two traps is crucial. The spiritual leads the way with the natural supplementing and supporting the work of the Spirit. One without the other is futile.

In this context of prayer-bathed strategic planning we developed a plan for a district-wide SWOT analysis (strengths, weaknesses, opportunities, threats), focus groups, listening forums, and strategic planning committees along with the guidance of our staff and presbytery. With the input of so many individuals, the phrase, *"Better Together"* depicted the heart of how we saw ourselves working to fulfill the mission and illustrate the means of fulfilling the vision God had given to us. As our people embraced my personal core values as what drives our endeavors, we find unity in opportunity of living out the reality of what it means to be *"Better Together."*

My team in the district office has enjoyed a great deal of consistency through the years. Individuals do transition from time to time, but maintaining the common threads that provide guidance in the long term, greatly aids the team development and provides a team culture that can be sustained through transitions.

MY CORE VALUES

- **The Supernatural** – everything begins and ends with God (prayer, spiritual gifts, spirit led, the miraculous)
- **Healthy Relationships** – ministry and life comes through relationship with God and others.
- **Effective Communication** – both through listening and sharing
- **Excellence in all things** – if something is worth doing, it is worth doing well.

Coaches and consultants sometimes differ on definition of terms like mission statements, vision and core values. I highly recommend to find someone that can step you and your team through this entire endeavor in order to develop a comprehensive strategic plan as you pursue God's dream for your team. My view of core values has become an anchor for me in our actions and plans.

For example, I have already expressed my commitment to prayer. But, is prayer a core value? No, prayer is what we do as the result of a core value. Then what is the core value? I am committed to prayer because of my core value of **The Supernatural**. God is my source of all I am. Prayer is a commitment because of my commitment to a healthy relationship with my God. The point is that, for me,

47

activities are not core values, but we do the action and activity because of our core values.

As you form your team and develop the members of your team, they need to understand why you do what you do, and that is based on your core values. If your actions don't reflect the realities of your core values, you should either rethink what your core values are so they are reflected by your actions or change what you do to be consistent with your core values. This ultimately results in your leadership being authentic for those you lead and those impacted by the ministry of your team.

You may want to pursue the following questions:

1. **What are your personal core values?**

_____

_____

2. **How will you discover your core values if you have not done so already?**

_____

_____

3. **What will be the results of implementing your core values in your ministry leadership?**

_____

_____

Chapter 5

HAT #3 - THE COACH'S HAT

When Jesus came to the region of Caesarea Philippi, he asked his disciples, "Who do people say the Son of Man is?"
(Matthew 16:13)

The final hat I have discovered in harnessing the power of teamwork is the coach's hat. Now before you jump to conclusions about what this hat might be, I'd like to paint another picture not associated with sports at all.

Television did not take up too much of my childhood. After all, I can still remember walking outside to the outhouse just to go to the bathroom. However, the shows I do remember watching and enjoying were old classic westerns such as Wagon Train, Gunsmoke, and, of course The Rifleman. My father was very selective about what we could watch on television. No Bonanza because it aired during the Sunday evening service and in those days there was no method to record the show. No I Love Lucy because it was too silly. I never could figure out why Wonder Woman was permitted! Go figure!!!

While it is tempting to go down memory lane, let me

49

focus. One of the common features depicted in westerns was the stage coach. The stage coach would come into town, drop people off, pick people up, deliver goods, and then continue on to the next town. Coaches take people from where they are, to where they need to be. These horse drawn coaches were a popular form of transportation.

Most often, the stage coach has a driver who doesn't have a name and is an undeveloped character in the story line. This is television. But in real life, he was an extremely important man. As you consider this new picture of what it means to be a coach, allow me to provide several reasons why this is a critical element to teamwork.

1. The stage coach driver determines who gets on!

Similarly, you determine who gets on your stage coach as well. Sometimes on purpose, other times by default. Have you ever wondered why some leaders seem to get all the really talented people? Perhaps you've thought to yourself, if I had her team, I could do what she's doing. A good question to ask yourself is: "What has God called me to do?"

For example, a missionary vision/call gets people on board. Those who are most effective in the itineration process communicate the vision for what God has called them to do in a clear and compelling way. Churches and individuals commit to prayer and financial support because they believe in the missionary's vision as well as their ability to fulfill the call God placed on their life. Your vision should do the same! It should draw people onto your team that will be part of the journey.

2. The stage coach driver checks the ticket.

Have people paid the price to get on, or are they willing to pay the price. Many people like to have positions without paying the price. Make sure those getting on your coach are willing to pay the price to get where you will lead them. If not, they're free-loaders and will contribute nothing but endless criticism and unsolicited suggestions. It is important to look at their previous experience and background and their potential to help the team.

3. **The stage coach driver knows where they're going and how to get there.**

When people attend your church, there is an underlining assumption that you know where you are going. No one would expect you to know all that will happen along the way, but it is expected of the leader to know where the group is going.

The difference between a manager and a leader is similar to the difference of the flight attendant and the pilot. People board the plane not because of the service or food. They board because they believe the pilot can get them from point A to point B. They trust the pilot to know where they're going and how to get there. Make no mistake, the role of a flight attendant is crucial. Never put down those who serve. Managing is important work. Leading is simply different.

Your position is a position of trust. They trust you to know where you're going. This is where the analogy ends. The stage coach driver knew the ways through the hills, the forests and away from potential dangers like hostile forces. Often times it feels as though the obstacles you encounter are dressed in flesh. Your obstacles may include the local zoning board, other religious establishments of even individuals you hoped would assist you on your journey. But remember, people are not your obstacle, they are the mission field. Obstacles will come your way, but if God has called you, He will lead you each step of the way.

The Apostle Paul ran into as much "people opposition" as any other minister in history. He was stoned, beaten, whipped, ship-wrecked, and persecuted at every turn. However, he is the same that scribed these words while under house arrest,

> *11 Put on the full armor of God, so that you can take your stand against the devil's schemes. 12 For our struggle is not against flesh and blood, but against the rulers, against the authorities, against the powers of this dark world and against the spiritual forces of evil in the heavenly realms. (Ephesians 6:11-12)*

4. The stage coach driver helps the right people get off.

Not everybody will take the full journey with you. Helping people off the coach and to their stop is one of the most gracious thing you can do. This may mean that you redirect people in ministry or positions. Unfortunately, some people just need to get off the stage coach.

Through the years I've had the pleasure of working with many wonderful people. Those that I've hired and brought into the inner circle have always been dear to my heart. Unfortunately, there have been times when I've needed to help them off the bus and begin the next leg of their journey. As a leader, you have the responsibility to help people figure out where they fit best, and help them discover their strengths. The mother bird will push the young bird out of the nest at the right time.

These decisions always cause me great stress. I anguished over each. Early on, I avoided those tough conversations. Instead of letting them off the bus, I kept them on much longer than I should have. Unfortunately I hurt the church, and I don't think I did them a favor either. I was entrusted with the authority to make that decision.

One responsibility a leader carries is helping others discover where they can best serve in the body of Christ. When a leader removes a member of the team out of personal frustration, anger or insecurity, that leader is not serving the best interest of the team. When a leader helps a team member realign themselves toward personal spiritual gifts, talents and passions, the leader is serving the best interest of the team member as well as the team. By valuing the team and the individual on the team, all are served, valued and affirmed. Unfortunately, everyone will not necessarily embrace these directions, but the leader who finds motivation through these principles can be confident of God's approval and favor because of the unselfish motives that prompt those decisions.

As the coach, you're responsibility is to move the team forward. Your team is depending on you. God has positioned you. Your effectiveness will be determined in large part by those you coach.

COACHING CULTURE

As you build your team, you will need to protect what God has entrusted to you. There are those who would derail you, hijack you, undermine your values and try to rewrite the culture of your team. You MUST protect your team. If you don't, no one else will.

AS THE LEADER OF YOUR TEAM, YOU SET THE CULTURE OF THE TEAM. The team will take on the personality of their coach. It is as if the coach transfuses his blood in his team. They take on his or her DNA. This is HUGELY IMPORTANT!!!

For many of you, you are setting a new culture. Establishing a new culture means wearing new "tracks" in the ground. It may be more bumpy in the beginning, but as the stage coach driver, you understand the need to be in the right set of tracks. Your tracks determine your destination.

It is this last point that is so critical for harnessing the power of the team, but it is also the most overlooked. You are the heartbeat of the team. God has placed you where you are because he knows what's in your heart. Your spiritual DNA is what will be transfused into the team.

Easier said than done... absolutely! Necessary? YOU BETTER BELIEVE IT! Without it, the power of the team is lost! Your heartbeat will dictate the speed of the team and will determine the compassion of your team. It delivers the moral ethics and work ethic of the team. With you, the team is better together!

The coaching concept provides significant tools for the leaders. Perhaps your mentor was more inclined to be a "teller" rather than an "asker." What do I mean by that? In many evangelical and Pentecostal circles, the biblical model of a prophet had dominated our methodology. There are many times and situations when "thus saith the Lord" is appropriate and needed. The coaching model helps provide an additional biblical model that is often very helpful.

Jesus often used questions, not just made statements, when dealing with his disciples. "Who do people say that I am?" and "Who do you say that I am?" are great examples of Jesus' teaching method using questions. The coach's hat utilizes this tool in helping others not only know the right answer, but also owning the truth. The disciples were able to declare for themselves, "Thou art the Christ, the son of the living God" rather than being told and expected to say amen to the truth.

Coaching your team gives them the opportunity of transitioning from being observers of what God is doing to being participants in what God is doing. To me, this is a critical point. Someone has stated this in the form of a question, "Is it better to do the work of 10 men or to get 10 men to do the work?" Obviously, "many hands make light work," to state another old proverb.

While none of this happens overnight, the quicker the team catches and embraces your heart, the greater the influence you have on the team's future. This is why the next chapter is so critical.

If your soul's DNA is to be transfused into the team… and your heartbeat become theirs… then one must make sure that what is being passed on is healthy and beneficial. A healthy team is only born from a healthy leader!

Like a father's child, they may look different, dress different, talk different, but their DNA… their blood line is the same.

Take a few minutes to reflect on the concept of how you coach your team. In addition, think about what value you may receive from having a coach to help you lead your team.

_____

_____

_____

_____

Part III
THE FUNCTION OF A TEAM
Emotional Intelligence, Teamwork and Change

Chapter 6

TEAMWORK AND
EMOTIONAL INTELLIGENCE

The heart of the discerning acquires knowledge,
for the ears of the wise seek it out.
(Proverbs 18:15)

I recently have taken up golf as a way to "relax," enjoy the outdoors, and also spend time with my son and grandsons. As a novice to the sport, I have discovered that the guys and gals on television make it look SO MUCH EASIER than it really is.

As I've tried to learn the sport, my son has been instructing me on how to use each club and different pointers about my swing. Tips such as, keep your head down, keep your hands low, swing through the ball, don't break your wrists and don't drop your back shoulder have all been helpful. However, it is extremely challenging to remember these all at the same time.

Leading a team is much like golf. There are so many moving parts that it feels like it is impossible to keep everything and everyone working in a natural, fluid motion.

The golf pros make it look easy. In life, as in golf, the discipline and consistent effort of each part functioning efficiently and effectively takes time and effort.

This is where the behavioral model of Emotional Intelligence "EI" or at times termed Emotional Quotient – "EQ" – is such a powerful concept when leading high performance teams.

The early EI theory was originally developed during the 1970's and 80's by the work and writings of psychologists Dr. Howard Gardner (Harvard), Dr. Peter Salovey (Yale) and Dr. John Mayer (New Hampshire). EI is increasingly relevant to organizational development and developing people because the EI principles provide a new way to understand and assess people's behaviors, management styles, attitudes, interpersonal skills, and potential. EI is an important consideration in human resources planning, job profiling, recruitment interviewing and selection, management development, customer relations, customer service, and more.

The EI concept argues that IQ, or conventional intelligence, is too narrow in scope; that there are wider areas of competencies that dictate and enable our success. Success requires more than IQ (Intelligence Quotient), which has tended to be the traditional measure of intelligence, ignoring essential behavioral and character elements. We've all met people who are academically brilliant and yet are socially and interpersonally inept. And we know that despite possessing a high IQ rating, success does not automatically follow.

This is the essential premise of EI -- to be successful requires effective awareness, control and management of one's own emotions, and those of other people. In other words, you don't have to be a straight "A" student to harness the power of teams. There are essential baseline requirements for various leadership levels, but the IQ is not the sole determiner of a leader's success.

Studies indicate that an individual's IQ remains relatively constant throughout life. A twenty year-old would not be expected to move from a 110 IQ to a 135 IQ. Your IQ is your IQ. The good new regarding your EI is that you can grow and develop your EI if you so desire and work on the required competencies. This means every leader, average or superior, can become a better leader of teams if so inclined. The more you learn about EI, the more you will come to grasp the significance of the discipline, and I hope you and your team will become *better together*.

There are 2 primary competencies that EI measures and teaches that assists CEO's, pastors, principals, etc. in which to lead their team effectively. The remainder of this chapter will review these two competencies and their application. Also, questions are provided that may provide insight and growth into your competencies and team leadership.

#1 PERSONAL COMPETENCY

The first of these two competencies is PERSONAL. Another term that might be helpful in clarifying these elements would be self-leadership. Most would agree, at least in theory, that we are not fit to lead others until we can lead ourselves. As such, Personal Competence determines how we manage ourselves.

Of all the biblical characters we find in Scripture, the one who best exemplifies growing in EI is Joseph. His story can be found in Genesis 37-50. We first encounter Joseph as the favorite son among many older brothers. His father, Jacob, spoiled him rotten at the exclusion of his siblings causing much rivalry among the boys. To top it off, in his teenage years he has two dreams given by the Lord, both describing him as ruling over his brothers. Even his father and mother bow down to him in the second dream.

We discover Joseph as a young 17 year old with lots of potential but not much savvy. Joseph has all the tools but isn't aware of how to use them (kind of like my golf game).

For the next 13 years Joseph faces one tragedy after another. He was assaulted by his brothers (near death), sold as a slave, became a servant in the home of a military leader in which he is accused (falsely) of raping the wife, and then thrown into Pharaoh's prison. While there, he helps another inmate by interpreting a dream, but Joseph is forgotten by him (the cupbearer to the king) once the cupbearer is released from prison.

If you're not familiar with the details of Joseph's story, I would encourage you to read it, then come back to this section. The details of developing the Personal Competencies are illustrated greatly in Joseph's life. According to Daniel Goldman in *Primal Leadership[11]*, Emotional Intelligence can be categorized into Personal Competencies and Social Competencies. The former being the foundation and prerequisite of the latter. The Personal Competencies are then understood to be comprised of Self-Awareness and Self-Management as follows:

A. Self-Awareness:

Knowing one's internal state, preferences, resources, and intuitions:

- *Emotional awareness:* Recognizing one's emotions and their effects

---

[11] Goleman, Daniel, Richard Boyatzis, & Annnie McKee. <u>Primal Leadership: realizing the power of emotional intelligence</u>. Boston, MA: Harvard Business School Press, 2002.

- *Accurate self-assessment:* Knowing one's strengths and limits
- *Self-confidence:* A strong sense of one's self-worth and capabilities

Prior to Joseph's education in the school of hard-knocks, he was not self-aware. He was, however, self-absorbed. When we are self-absorbed, it actually interferes with our leadership of self and others. It can be described as only caring about and interested in oneself.

Self-awareness allows an individual to be confident and allows us to see our lives in context of the world around us.

QUESTIONS TO CONSIDER

1. **What emotions do I experience on a regular basis? What are their triggers?**

_____

_____

_____

2. How do these emotions affect my leadership or attitude toward others.

_____

_____

_____

3. Where is a safe place I can process my emotions? What do I do with negative emotions?

_____

_____

_____

4. What strengths do I have to offer others (specifically my team)?

_____

_____

_____

5. What limits do I have personally and in relationship to my leadership of the team?

_____

_____

_____

B. Self-Management

Managing one's internal state, impulses, and resources

- *Self-control:* Keeping disruptive emotions and impulses in check
- *Trustworthiness:* Maintaining standards of honesty and integrity
- *Conscientiousness:* Taking responsibility for personal performance
- *Adaptability:* Flexibility in handling change
- *Innovation:* Being comfortable with novel ideas, approaches, and new information

After Joseph's 13 years of slavery and imprisonment, he is called upon to interpret the dream of the most powerful man on the earth, the leader of Egypt... Pharaoh. Soon thereafter, he would lead the entire nation of Egypt and manage all the providences on behalf of the Pharaoh.

This once impulsive, entitled boy of a small tribe had learned Self-Management through his disappointments, abandonments, loneliness, and betrayal. No longer did circumstances rule over Joseph; Joseph ruled his circumstances through the competency of Self-Management.

QUESTIONS TO CONSIDER:

1. How do I handle difficult people, and emotionally charged situations?

_____

_____

_____

2. When was the last time you received useful feedback from your team? What did they tell you that allowed you to lead more effectively?

_____

_____

_____

3. How do you typically respond to changes and innovations? What new ideas have you embraced and implemented in the last 12 months?

_____

_____

_____

It becomes evident in a story like Joseph's why Personal Competencies of Self-Awareness and Self-Management go hand in hand with Social Competencies. When one is unaware of how one's personal emotions and expressions affect others, relational tension often results. In order to exercise influence, integrity must be established in the heart of a leader and evident to the team. Growing and expanding your EI allows you to harness the power of teamwork!

As you look to harness the power of your team working together, a great deal will depend on your ability to develop these Personal Competencies in your life, and leadership. Schedule time to take an honest assessment of these areas, and discover ways in which you might take some next steps to improving the leadership of your team.

To be self-aware means you recognize your own emotions, positive and negative, healthy and unhealthy. When that is true, you are more able to respond to those emotions and begin managing them in healthy ways. As followers of Jesus, we identify that as developing and growing in our character. It allows us to also grow in the Social Competencies.

#2 SOCIAL COMPETENCIES:

The ability to understand your own emotional state provides a foundation for understanding the emotions of others which, in turn, is a critical piece within the context of leading a team. EI recognizes the reality of relationships, especially when applied to team leadership. The team leader who has developed Social Competencies demonstrates the capabilities of both Social Awareness and Relational Management as described below and is comprised of three competencies.

A. Social Awareness

Recognition and the ability to deal with other's emotions is Social Awareness.

- *Empathy:* The ability to understand someone else's feelings and experience them through active listening, focus on the task/goal without conflict, and maneuvering through emotional boundaries.
- *Organizational Awareness:* The ability to read the current of emotions and political/relational realities in your group or team.
- *Service Orientation:* Built from your empathy, assisting other's personal development and satisfaction.

QUESTIONS TO CONSIDER:

1. **Identify key team members and their current experience in the team you lead. What emotions are surfacing?**

_____

_____

_____

2. **What emotional realities are your team facing in the life of your organization as a whole (beyond your team)?**

_____

_____

_____

Joseph struggled with this competency early on in his life. As he shared both his dreams, first with his brothers, and the later with the whole family, he was seemingly unware of how it would affect them. It wasn't until he went through the school of *hard-knocks* that the Lord was able to develop these into his life.

B. **Relationship Management**

Using your awareness of your own emotions and that of others to build strong and effective relationships and teamwork.

- *Influence:* the ability to win and persuade people to your viewpoint or common tasks or goal.
- *Leadership:* Your team is willing to follow your lead and wants to work with you to meet goals.
- *Developing Others:* Observing and recognizing opportunities to develop individuals on your team, and team skills as a whole.
- *Communication:* Being persuasive, objective and poised well in the emotional context of the exchanged and the ability to appreciate other's view points and contributions.

- *Change Catalyst:* Someone who seeks out and initiates new ideas and approaches
- *Conflict Management:* The ability to identify, prevent or navigate areas of conflict toward a positive outcome.
- *Teamwork & Collaboration:* An aptitude in creating a cohesive team by ensuring the objective is understood by all, aligning behaviors toward a common end, and demonstrates that they value all contributions.

QUESTIONS TO CONSIDER:

1. **In the last 6 months, how have you helped your team build a sense of togetherness and closeness? How can you improve this quality in the next 3 months?**

_____

_____

_____

2. **What is your current strategy in developing your team? What specific skills or experience will they need to be successful?**

_____

_____

_____

3. **Name the top 3 goals for your team? If you can clarify, how were those goals established, by you or in an open team context? How might you involve your team in creating goals for the next year?**

_____

_____

_____

By the time we find Joseph in the final chapters of Genesis, he has grown from a self-absorbed teenager, to a leader of a world power. We see his growth not only in his work as Pharaoh's representative, but also in his interaction when his brothers finally are exposed to his true identity. His maturity provided the atmosphere for healing and reconciliation to take place.

The above outline on Emotional Intelligence and its impact on team leadership was taken and adapted from Daniel Goleman's book, _Primal Leadership_, as sited earlier. If you would like to learn more on this subject, I strongly recommend beginning with his work first, and then expanding from there. You can also find resources for further study at the end of this book.

Chapter 7

TEAMWORK AND
CULTURAL CHANGE

When the day of Pentecost came,
they were all together in one place.
(Acts 2:1)

I've shared with you through these previous chapters much about my own experiences and lessons learned. The reason is that everyone's individual journey matters. Leadership is as much about WHO you are as WHAT you do! The integrity of the leader is about the integration of the leader holistically, emotionally, physically, relationally, and spiritually!

You see… God doesn't recruit you for your skills, your charisma, your looks, or your potential. He recruits you to His Kingdom work so you can be a vessel He can flow through. Understanding yourself, becoming a better team leader, and increasing your Emotional Intelligence are great tools for the utility belt, a willing and open vessel is the

Lord's #1 requirement.

This is important for every pastor to understand. You said YES to the Lord's recruitment invitation long before you ever said YES to a local congregation, ministry, or organization. It is not just important to remember this for effectiveness sake, but it will also affect your impact on the next topic at hand: Teamwork and Cultural Change.

FIRST THINGS FIRST

Let's begin with culture and change, before we discover how to harness the power of teamwork in the process of cultural change. Changing the culture of an organization is messy business. In order to keep your hands and heart clean, there are a few things to remember and apply.

1. **Stay anchored in the Word and in Prayer**: We must not substitute creativity, innovation, education or accommodation for the work of the Spirit in people's lives. And there is no substitute to God's Spirit working in your life.

2. **Resist the urge to conform**: It is more natural for the culture to change us rather than us to change the culture. The path of least resistance is always appealing, but most often leads to the waterfall. You are the leader because you are called to turn the tide.

3. **Find the balance between confrontation and accommodation**: Not everything can be changed at once. Those in the medical community understand the need to stabilize the patient before major surgery is performed. As a vice-president for a television station outside of New York City once outlined for me: "Stabilize – Organize – Mobilize" in that order.

4. **Know and understand the language of the culture**: The best way to do this is to hear the story of many people. Hear their story from many different angles and persuasions. Their narrative will describe their culture, both healthy and dysfunctional. Be sure to strengthen the positive, and identify the unhealthy aspects. Putting a label (axioms are a good idea to use here) on both the positive and negative allow others to see what you are seeing.

PIECES OF A HEALTHY CULTURE

Peter Drucker has been credited with the statement "Culture eats strategic planning for lunch." As important as planning may be, culture can easily render ineffective any plan that may be developed. Cultural change is complex and often filled with unexpected detours. Cultural change is about painting a different structure. How do we go about leading cultural change? How do we paint a different structure, when the current structure is unhealthy or ineffective? Below are 4 pieces of the puzzle that are necessary for cultural change to occur in your team, church or organization.

Piece #1: PRAY

Don't skip this one, just because you think you know about prayer

From Moses, to Daniel, to Nehemiah, the common thread among each of these spiritual leaders is they prayed. They heard from the Lord, they encountered the Almighty. Their confidence was not in self, but in the Mighty Hand of God that was upon them.

For every great leader in the Bible, prayer marked their launch into God's work and prayer sustained them in the midst of their assignment. If you and I are to make a spiritual impact in the church or the world, our spiritual power comes only through prayer. Prayer, true presence based prayer, feeds the anointing and calling of the Lord upon our lives.

However, what is often overlooked is that each of these leaders assembled teams that prayed and believed God as well. We see the prophet Daniel's influence when we read of the 3 young Hebrew boys who would not bow to an idol, and of Daniel's reputation for praying three times a day, NO MATTER WHAT! Nehemiah consistently refocused the entire nation that returned to Jerusalem to call upon and rely upon the Lord their God.

It is not enough for a team leader to be a man or woman of prayer, they must lead their teams to experience God for themselves, and learn to trust God in prayer as well. The power of teamwork is witnessed in the power of *prayer-work*.

1. How has God already burdened your heart in prayer?

_____

_____

_____

_____

2. When might you steal away time to spend with God in the next 4 weeks, specifically asking him to reveal His desires for you and your church? Where would you go?

_____

_____

_____

3. What opportunities exists (or could exists) to involve your team and those you are leading to a deeper level of prayer?

_____

_____

_____

Piece #2: PREPARE

Prepare Yourself – be ready to change. Every church I've pastored, or position I've held has required something different from me. I have personally had to grow, rethink, adapt, and transform each time God has put me someplace different. As your church grows and changes, understand you'll need to change with it. What my wife needed from me when we were married at 21 years of age, is quite different from what she needs from me today. Prepare to be changed! The areas we are most often changed and affected involve our Heart, Mind, Soul, and Strength. How might God be preparing you or desire to prepare you in each of these four areas? What steps can you begin to take this week in cooperation with God?

1. HEART (your Passions):

_____

_____

2. MIND (your Intellect):

_____

_____

3. SOUL (your Emotions & Relations):

_____

_____

4. STRENGTH (your Physical Body):

_____

_____

Prepare your Team – You don't like to be surprised and neither does your team. Make sure they are seeing the urgency of the needs, and are asking the right questions before you lead them to the solutions and answers. You may not need your team's permission, but you need your team's buy-in. Take the time to prepare them relationally, mentally, and spiritually. If you don't do the work of hoeing the ground, you can't do the work of sowing the seed.

1. **What conversations do you need to have with a team member which would take place outside of a regularly scheduled team meeting that would have positive results?**

---

2. **Are there any attitudes or values surfacing that need to be addressed because of their toxic nature to the team? What is their origin (not who)?**

Piece #3: PLAN

As a leader, you must plan your priorities and prioritize your plans. Without planning, you become the slave to everyone with a good idea. Perhaps you have worked for the person who goes away to a conference, comes back with the newest idea and now the church has to turn directions. Six months later, the leader goes to another conference, returns and has a new direction. This leader not only frustrates the team God has brought around them, but may cause di-vision (multiple visions) for the organization.

The plans you and your team make should come from your Critical Success Factors. A critical success factor is "a management term for an element that is necessary for an organization or project to achieve its mission.

It is a **critical factor** or activity required for ensuring the **success** of a company or an organization.[12]" Many leaders and teams are unsure of what factors will determine their success.

Discovering and defining one's Critical Success Factors and that of your teams are a key component for harnessing the power of teamwork. It allows your team and each individual to work with focus and purpose. Each team that you lead will have a different set of factors that should be clearly defined. Whether it is serving on a board, a worship team, kids church, or pastoral staff, each team has different set of factors that determine their success.

If you are a senior leader, I would encourage you to take a few moments to think and answer the following questions:

1. What are your personal Critical Success Factors? These factors are things only you can or should do.

- _____

- _____

- _____

- _____

- _____

---

[12] https://en.wikipedia.org/wiki/Critical_success_factor

2. **What are the teams you have direct involvement with? Begin with the 3 most influential teams you are currently working with.**

- TEAM #1_____

- TEAM #2_____

- TEAM #3_____

3. **List the purpose of their existence and how they contribute to the forward movement of the organization. List the team "name" and clarify a minimum of 4 critical success factors for each team.**

TEAM NAME   4 CRITICAL SUCCESS FACTORS

_____   _____

                  _____

                  _____

                  _____

_____   _____

                  _____

                  _____

                  _____

_____   _____

              _____

              _____

              _____

_____   _____

              _____

              _____

              _____

Once you, along with your team (it is best if your team is a part of the discovery process to assure by-in and ownership), determine the Critical Success Factors, then effective planning can begin. The 4-6 Factors allow you to schedule what is most important, and will make you most effective. Your team will be empowered and energized when their purpose and plans align. As team leader, you help them harness that power!

Piece #4: POSITION

Finally, I want to mention Position. Specifically, how to position yourself for the blessing. In God's kingdom positioning yourself is a posture of the heart. While some may choose to try political maneuvers, or attempt to manipulate circumstance to gain position, jobs, or access; positioning in the Kingdom of God is a verb, not a noun. We position ourselves through prayer, worship, serving, giving, etc... Remember the words of Christ, "... whoever wants to become great among you much be your servant."

Some of the greatest players in NBA history were marked by their ability to rebound (Shaquille O'Neal, Charles Barkley, and Carl Malone). Rebounding is less about athletic ability, and more about getting in the right position before you need to be there. You position yourself to get the rebound, even before the shot hits the rim.

The same goes for some of the great shooters. Some of the best shooters in the NBA's history were not the most athletic (i.e., Larry Bird, Reggie Miller, John Paxton) but they knew how to get open at the right time. They moved without the ball, ran the floor, and learned the system of the team's offense. The shots they made were the last step in the whole process. Get into position... get your team into position, so when God throws you the ball, you're ready to hit the shot.

Three of the greatest positions Jesus spoke of are listed in Matthew chapter 6. He says, "When you give..." (v. 2), "When you pray..." (v. 5), "And when you fast..." (v. 16). These three activities position our heart in a place where God loves to respond. Giving, Praying and Fasting position us to receive a blessing that we might be a blessing.

1. **How might you position yourself in the next season of life and ministry?**

_____

_____

2. **In what ways is this type of positioning different than what you're used to?**

_____

_____

FINAL THOUGHT

Culture includes both what your team believes, as well as how they behave. As always, actions speak louder than words. This is why it takes an astute leader to evaluate, and change culture. We, along with our teams, must be personally affected, challenged and committed to establishing a healthy culture through Prayer, Preparation, Planning, and Positioning.

Why have I spent so much time on these four areas as it relates to culture? Because, above all else, your church should be spiritual in nature not just some secular organizational structure to produce a crowd of people on a Sunday morning. Culture is the unseen, behind the scene way your team functions. Be sure your culture is grounded on the spiritual principles that create health for your team.

Just one more side comment on this… Culture is liquid and shifting. This is both the good news and the challenge. If you are moving from a sick (unproductive) culture to a healthy (productive) culture, then things can change and shift. It will take much time and effort from you and your team, but it can and must happen.

However, once you establish a healthy culture, know that culture is never static. The team leader must be vigilant in protecting culture and enculturating new team members. Nothing stays the same forever, nor should it. Because of the fluid state of team leadership, the remaining chapters describe the characteristics and skill necessary for long-term team success.

Part IV
THE FULFILLMENT OF A TEAM

Where REAL Leadership Meets REAL Life

Chapter 8

THE CHALLENGES OF A TEAM

How good and pleasant it is when
God's people live together in unity!
(Psalm 133:1)

Almost every year Marjie and I try to take a vacation with our two children and their families. It has proven to be one of the best investments we've ever made in our family. The memories we have stored and the time spent with our greatest investment (our kids and our grandkids) have been well worth our effort.

At one such recent vacation we journeyed down to Florida and visited Disney World and some of the other parks. We had the opportunity of attending a 4D movie taken from the animated movie "A Bugs Life." I had been to a number of 3D movies in which the action on the screen seemed to move off the screen and come to our seats. But this movie took it a step further. The special effects had wind blowing in your face. The stinkbug sprayed a nasty smell. They also had what felt like a little stinger in the back of each seat so when the bees flew around with the 3D animation, it felt like you got stung or poked in your back. It was quite amazing and it felt very real.

4D is the inclusion of technology which attempts to make the fake or imaginary more real. But when it comes to team leadership dynamics, the 4-D's we will discuss in this chapter, are as real as it gets. The skills, spiritual stability, and emotional intelligence we've examined all come into play simultaneously.

Your team, each individual member, as well as the team leader them self, will inevitably face these 4-D's. How they handle them are paramount for long-term individual and team success. In fact, I've become convinced that it is less about what we do with the 4-D's and more about what they do to us. Here they are:

- **Discouragement**
- **Disappointment**
- **Disagreement**
- **Disengagement**

I like the analogy of the captain of a ship on the high seas being compared to the leader of a team. There is not a great deal of skill required of the captain as long as the weather is calm and there are no obstacles to challenge the direction of the ship. Facing the storms on the journey of leadership requires knowledge, skills and competencies that can be gained through training, preparation and experience. Storms will come and challenges will be faced, but how you deal with those challenges will determine you and your team's success.

How will you as a leader handle those storms? It is not a matter of *if the storms will come*, but a matter of *when*. Perhaps there is another way to deal with the storms. What if the captain sees the storms coming on the horizon and adjusts the course of the ship around the storm in order to avoid much of the effects of the winds and waves? The experienced leader will do likewise. Not all winds or waves can be avoided, but minimizing their impact on the team can greatly assist the leader to guide his team safely and effectively through and around the challenges that will inevitably come.

Let's look at each D you will inevitably face and need to lead your team through, in order to harness the power of teamwork in your context.

NAVIGATING THE 4-D'S

A leader does not always have the convenience of possessing all the desired quantifiable facts from which to make accurate assessments and informed decisions. Like the 4D movie, the leader will probably "feel" what is going on, even if he cannot always put his finger on the exact issue that precipitates the challenge being faced. Your emotional intelligence will help in feeling your way through these times of uncertainty. If you have established the foundation of the personal competencies of self-assessment and self-management, then you will have greater success at dealing with the social competencies. Understanding how others are seeing the context of your leadership team's efforts enables you as the leader to not be as defensive or take these 4-D issues as personal attacks or rejection, but allows you to understand where these issues are coming from and enables you to more effectively handle them. We start with discouragement.

DISCOURAGEMENT

Discouragement can have its origin from any number of both internal and external sources. Individuals face many personal issues in their lives from financial pressures to health concerns to relational upheaval. The team leader has little ability to negate those issues just because he is the team leader. Knowing what your team members are facing in their personal lives helps to understand them and patiently nurture them through their personal crisis. Wishing the drama wasn't there does not remove the drama. Accept that reality and move forward. There may be times when the individual's issues will limit the effectiveness of the team, but remember the values you hold dear and care for the people in your life, not just the task you are endeavoring to fulfill.

Discouragement regarding the functioning of the team is a different matter. Many times this occurs because there are inappropriate expectation. Comparison to others will inevitably lead to discouragement. One family we ministered to was constantly comparing our church to a church their family attended years prior. The wife would often begin a sentence, "at our previous church." In time I asked her about that church and she explained that it was made up of 30 people and eventually closed.

Why was I fretting over a closed church? Why would I try to emulate an unsuccessful spiritual community? Comparison takes our eyes off what we have control over, and imagines results without the process. Below are a few suggestions to holding discouragement at bay, and energizing you team:

- Provide a well-defined set of roles and goals
- Privately and publicly recognize productive behavior and efforts
- Encourage people before they need encouragement
- Keep the vision constantly before your teams
- Share team wins on a regular basis
- Motivate your team with fresh challenges

- Directly confront the "dark-clouds" in your team.

Teams are never productive when discouragement overtakes them. Take a few moments and evaluate your team and each members.

1. **What discouraging events have happened in your life or your team's lives in last 12 months?**

_____

_____

_____

2. **To what extent has "comparison" become part of your team's culture? What effects have that comparison had on your team?**

_____

_____

_____

3. **In what ways can you actively encourage your team?**

_____

_____

_____

DISAPPOINTMENT

Disappointment is the second of the 4-D's. While disappointment is very similar to discouragement, it takes on the added quality of not having attained the desired goal. Sometimes those goals are for team performance, relational expectations, or those that we serve not delivering on what we expected from them. Disappointments are dangerous because they potentially can cause your team (or you) to not try again and avoid taking risks.

The first church we pastored was a small congregation of about fifty people. I felt the Lord wanted to bless our small congregation and I wanted to include the people in the effort to see us grow. My goal was for us to have 100 people in church on Easter Sunday. I shared with the congregations that I would grow a beard. If we had a hundred people on Easter Sunday I would keep the beard and if not I would shave it off. Looking back I wondered what motivation I was giving to those who didn't like beards. Regardless, we had over 100 there on that amazing Sunday morning, and quite frankly, I have had some sort of facial hair ever since. It worked! PTL!

We saw good things happen as a result and God blessed. There have been other times when we set out to reach a goal and didn't make it. For instance, at another church we were raising funds for building project. I believed we could raise the money in one year's time. Three years later, we finally approached our goal. Needless to say, I felt very frustrated and disappointed along the way. As the team leader, though, I had to speak life and keep us moving forward. I could not allow the team to get lost in the forest of disappointment.

I have a very good pastor friend that has helped me during this time. To help visualize the progress we were making, we made a poster (this was before electronic computer generated graphics) with a thermometer drawn on it indicating our progress. The thermometer was colored in from the bottom, moving upward as if your temperature was rising. We eventually reached our goal but it seemed to take forever. No one told me they were disappointed when week after week the red did not seem to be moving very much, but I can tell you I was!

My friend helped me in this way. Their church was raising money for a building program too. Rather than setting one goal (don't remember the actual numbers), they set multiple goals. The first was a victory goal (a manageable number), next was a faith goal, then an overcomer goal and finally an ultimate goal. The amount was not as important as the congregation having progressive goals that would stretch their faith while also not setting them up for disappointment.

Further, try to not confuse goals with vision. Vision is the big picture of what God wants to do. It is a picture of God's preferred future for you and your ministry. At times I have shared my vision for PennDel as the rising tide where all ships are elevated because of what God is doing. Goals are the incremental steps we take toward that vision as the Lord directs each step we take. "Unless the Lord builds the house they labor in vain who build it[13]." Realistic goals toward God's vision helps to minimize disappointment among the members of our team (and us) and keep us moving full speed ahead.

What goals are you and your team currently working toward? How clear are your team-members about these goals? Could they list them clearly? How are they attached to the larger vision?

Attempt to make a distinction between your goals and

---

[13] Psalm 127:1

your vision in the space below:

VISION   **GOALS**

_____   _____

_____   _____

_____   _____

_____   _____

_____   _____

_____   _____

_____   _____

_____   _____

_____   _____

_____   _____

_____   _____

DISAGREEMENT

The third of the 4 Ds is disagreement. As is true with discouragement and disappointment, disagreement can be anchored in many different areas. Some people choose to be the cause of division and turmoil in whatever situation they find themselves. Disagreement left unchecked or swept under the rug will eventually turn into division. Disagreement is natural, division will is a culture killer.

A person that disagrees with you will more likely turn into a person who causes division when those disagreements are swept under the rug and not dealt with in a mature, direct way. However, some people are committed to causing division no matter how well you deal with disagreements.

A team leader must be aware of persons that are described in Kenneth C. Haugk's book, *Antagonist in the Church*. Antagonists are not interested in any win-win arrangement. Their issue is with anyone in the senior level authority. While a leader should never rejoice when individuals leave the team, quite honestly, antagonist need to leave the team and the church. As the writer of Proverbs states in 26:20 "Without wood a fire goes out; without gossip a quarrel dies down." Love, but don't chase the fuel of the fires.

As long as a person whose character is defective is part of the team, no leader will be able to lead a healthy organization. Sadly, there are times when you must decide who should be on your team and who should not. When faced with these issues, prayerfully consider what action should be taken. Consider that your critic may be right and the division could be because of your leadership, skills, or character, but after examining your own heart, know that there are wolves out there in sheep's clothing.

Your role as a leader is the protection of the flock. If you guard yourself against just protecting yourself and your own interest and make the sheep your priority, this safeguards your heart and ensures proper motivation rather than manipulation and self-justification.

Another major cause of disagreement that leads to division deals with values. A team leader is to be sure your team members are committed to shared values. We sometimes ask if we are on the same page. What does that mean? For me, the core values are those core commitments that the group feels deep within themselves about which they are unwilling to compromise.

Compromise is not a bad word in many situations. A husband and wife compromise on the type of car to buy, the color of carpet in the living room, sometimes how many kids they want. You should not be willing to compromise your core values. Individually and as a group you choose to commit to certain principles or standards. Everything that is done is then measured against your core values.

The astute leader will know and respond to disagreement differently than division. While they begin similar, their effect is drastically different.

1. **Are there any difficult decisions you have been delaying, that may jeopardize the unity, vision, and potential impact your team can make? Are there any teammates that are toxic to the team?**

_____

_____

_____

_____

2. **How would you define your team or organization's Core Values?**

_____

_____

_____

_____

DISENGAGEMENT

The final of the 4 Ds is Disengagement, the act or process of withdrawing from involvement and relationship. The leader is wise to use emotional intelligence skills to monitor their team. Effectively connecting the members to efforts of the team is critical to keeping them engaged.

Effective communication is the key. This must include both verbal and non-verbal communication. For example, I can tell you we want everyone to feel welcome in our church service, but when no one personally welcomes a new guest, or shakes their hands, or show them where their kids will be for kids' church, then non-verbal communication speaking very loudly.

I am grateful for my wife for many different reasons, one of which is that she helps me to be more sensitive to what others are hearing from me and our ministries. Your spouse is a gift of God and if you are single, develop relationships that will be able and willing to keep you accountable and tell you the hard truth in love.

Ultimately, I have three rules for helping others not become disengaged: 1. communicate, 2. communicate, 3. communicate. When you get tired of sharing the vision, figure out a way to share it in a fresher way. When you think everyone understands your core values and embraces them, talk with a few trusted friends and say it again in a new way. Provide connection points in ways that you identify with and then in ways you have no interest in. Not everyone thinks like you and not everyone will respond the same way you do.

Shortly after becoming superintendent of the Pennsylvania-Delaware District, our Presbytery invited several of our younger ministers to come to talk with us about how we could more effectively serve their needs. One of our younger ministers stated, respectfully but candidly, that we just expect them to come to the district events. I agreed that was true. You see, my generation attends the organizational events out of loyalty to the fellowship, period. He proceeded to say how they are constantly receiving information from all kinds of organizations telling them how great these other organization events will be. We, on the other hand, just expect them to come because we announce the event. I will tell you that was a moment of illumination for me. I realized how true that was. As a result, we have endeavored to develop materials, print, video, online, snail mail, etc. to communicate our events and the value they will bring to our people. I am sure we can and will continue to improve, but communication helps to avoid disengagement that is so unhealthy to an organization and teams.

THE OUTCOME OF 4-D TEAMWORK

Teamwork is a true 4-D experience. It touches us emotionally, relationally, physically, and spiritually. Teams that face these elements and come out the other side are strengthened by the fact that they have overcome. Embrace the 4-D's as the pathway for you and your team to become potent and powerful.

What your team gains in the journey is *confidence* in one another, *faith* in God who has seen them through, and *perspective* of the fears and dangers they've encountered along the way. Most team members who have experienced these and overcome, look back with a fondness toward the relationships developed and the personal growth they underwent, and what they were able to accomplish in spite of the challenges. They love being a part of a team which has harnessed the power of teamwork.

Chapter 9

THE BODY OF TEAMWORK

Even so the body is not made up
of one part but of many.
(1 Corinthians 12:14)

Many years ago when finances were very tight, we received a great deal on a short vacation through a perspective time-share. The catch... we had to listen to their sales pitch. (I hate these sales pitches!) The gal assigned to us as the company representative was very pleasant and not pushy at all. We went through the usual dialogue of where we liked to vacation, how much we spend each year staying at hotels, and the annual cost of those stays and how much we projected to spend over the next few decades.

As we talked our guide revealed more and more about herself. She was single and did not want anyone to tie her down or limit her ability to do what she wanted to do. You could tell she was very proud of her position in life and was determined to live for herself. As she talked, she revealed she grew up in a "strict" church environment. To her, God would limit her choices and take away her freedom to do as she pleased. Work was the same. No restrictions, encumbrances, or accountability to anyone but herself. If the team served her purposes, fine. If not, she would not have been on the team. She preferred to be a team of one.

As a follower of Jesus, working together under the Lordship of Christ provides a natural model of being a member of a team. Just as you cannot do church alone, neither can you effectively serve God to your fullest capacity as a loner. We need each other, just as an eye needs the hands or feet. Scripture illustrates the interdependence of members of the body which is an ideal metaphor of working together as a team. We can work through the implications of Paul's discourse on harnessing the power of teamwork as found in 1 Corinthians 12:12-27[14].

UNITY WITHOUT UNIFORMITY

12 Just as a body, though one, has many parts, but all its many parts form one body, so it is with Christ. 13 For we were all baptized be one Spirit so as to form one body— whether Jews or Gentiles, slave or free—and we were all given the one Spirit to drink. 14 Even so the body is not made up of one part but of many.

The first principle we see listed in Paul's discourse is that of unity. The quickest way to weaken the team is through disunity. That which threatens a team is also that which provide its power. This element is DIVERSITY.

Paul says that there are many parts, but these parts need to form one body. One in movement, one is purpose, one in direction. The bigger the vision, the more parts are needed. Each part does not need to be like the others.

Being "baptized by one Spirit" is a critical element when it comes to team dynamics. The team leader needs to pay great attention to the "soul" of their team. Interestingly enough, even if you don't find yourself as the official leader

---

[14] Adapted from Jason Tourville's Discipleship Training Materials, unpublished, "Starting Line".

of the team, you can greatly affect the unity of the team. For any team, unity is the soul of the team.

1. **What does my team rally around? Is there a common vision, or goal?**

_____

_____

_____

2. **Are there any difficult conversations you have been putting off that may be threatening the unity of the team?**

_____

_____

_____

DEFINED VALUE

[15] Now if the foot should say, "Because I am not a hand, I do not belong to the body," it would not for that reason stop being part of the body. [16] And if the ear should say, "Because I am not an eye, I do not belong to the body," it would not for that reason stop being part of the body. [17] If the whole body were an eye, where would the sense of hearing be? If the whole body were an ear, where would the sense of smell be? [18] But in fact God has placed the parts in the body, every one of them, just as he wanted them to be. [19] If they were all one part, where would the body be? [20] As it is, there are many parts, but one body.

From the Old to the New Testament the God of the Bible ascribes value to those who follow His voice. From Moses, to King David, to Peter, God provides value and purpose to His people. In fact, He often renames them according to their value and purpose (i.e., Abram-Abraham, Sarai-Sarah Jacob-Israel, Cephas-Peter/Rock, and Saul-Paul).

These examples are important when it comes to teamwork. As a team leader, it is your responsibility to provide defined value to each team member. Defined roles and responsibility empowers your team to know how they matter to the team. To use the Apostle's analogy, the "foot" is just as important as the "hand." However, your team needs you to define the value of what they can bring to the "body".

Not only should roles be clearly defined, but as God "placed the parts in the body, every one of them, just as he wanted them to be..." so a team leader should place teammates in the proper role to succeed. Position your people for success. As those you lead discover value and purpose, a beneficial outcome is that they tend to value the other members when they understand what each person brings to the team.

The 2015 NBA championships witnessed the rise of the Golden State Warriors. The team was led by a baby faced player by the name of Steph Curry. His size is not intimidating, nor is his leadership overwhelmingly dominate. That being said, Steph apparently is very secure in who he is as a person and a player. This confidence allows the other teammates to embrace their roles. Andre Iguodala (A.I.) was traded to the Warrior in 2014. At the time he was in the prime of his career, 2-times named to the NBA All-Defensive Team, and a gold-medalist in the 2012 Olympics. One title that had alluded him to this point was the NBA Championship.

Upon joining the Warriors, their coach, Steve Kerr, asked A.I. to come off the bench as the teams 6th man. The NBA is known for big egos and big salaries and most players/millionaires would not have accepted this new role. However, Kerr told his superstar that this change would help the team win the title. A.I. accepted his new role.

Because of the on-the-court leadership of Curry, the bench leadership of Kerr, and the team-first mentality of Andre, the Golden State Warriors became the national champs. At the end of the series, there was an interesting turn of event. Instead of Steph Curry as the best player, the highest scorer, and the face of the franchise receiving the coveted MVP of the series, that honor went to Andre Iguodala. It was beautiful to see Steph celebrate his teammates recognition, and to hear Andre give the best compliment I've ever heart by an MVP, "I want to be just like Steph when I grow up. Just a God-fearing man... a great guy."

Defined Value became a key ingredient to team's success. Of course this was not Coach Steve Kerr's first experience with a championship team. He won 3-titles with the Chicago Bulls with the legendary Michael Jordan, and epic coach Phil Jackson. He also picked up 2 more titles with the epitome of team play, the San Antonio Spurs. This year they broke the NBA record of team win record at 73-9 (previously held by the Bulls), but came up a bit short of the Championship title, losing to Cleveland in seven games.

1. **What roles might need to be clarified for team members:**

_____

_____

2. **How does the team know the roles of the other members? How can I place each teammate operates in their sweet spot?**

_____

_____

3. **Do any of our teammates need to be shifted around in order to better function?**

_____

_____

LOVING ACCEPTANCE

> [21] The eye cannot say to the hand, "I don't need you!" And the head cannot say to the feet, "I don't need you!" [22] On the contrary, those parts of the body that seem to be weaker are indispensable, [23] and the parts that we think are less honorable we treat with special honor. And the parts that are unpresentable are treated with special modesty, [24] while our presentable parts need no special treatment. But God has put the body together, giving greater honor to the parts that lacked it, [25] so that there should be no division in the body, but that its parts should have equal concern for each other. [26] If one part suffers, every part suffers with it; if one part is honored, every part rejoices with it.
>
> [27] Now you are the body of Christ, and each one of you is a part of it.

The Apostle Paul ends his discourse on spiritual teamwork shifting focus from what God does by bringing a church together, or even what a team leader does and addresses how teammates (members of the body) relate to one another.

In the verses preceding, Paul addresses insecurities team members might feel "Because I am not a hand, I do not belong to the body." In this final suggestion he describes the loving acceptance each member should have for one another, "The eye cannot say to the hand, 'I don't need you!'" Although teammates are often very different, accepting one another with love is what releases the power of teamwork. Without loving acceptance, there is just tolerance. Tolerance only lasts until conflict arises.

We read in verse 25 that the opposite of division is care and concern. The moment we care for the needs, feelings and overall well-being of those in the "body," or on our team, in our family, or another place, there is no room for division. Loving acceptance is the antidote to a divisive atmosphere.

For team leaders, when troubles arise, this is the opportunity to bring your team together and integrate loving acceptance into the DNA of your team. Below are 5 opportunities every leader has to build a culture of loving acceptance:

1. **Personal Difficulties:** When a team member is going through a personal difficulty (illness, loss, etc...), this is a time to bring the team together and rally around that person. Sometimes the team can help change the circumstances, other times it is the proverbial "group hug" that communicates... "WE'RE WITH YOU!!!"

2. **External Opposition:** Sports teams, and professional athletes are constantly looking for external motivation. They use articles written, commentators' words, and opposing team's cutting remarks as motivation. The reason External Opposition creates a culture of loving acceptance is that it makes your work/ministry personal. It sparks the competitive drive in us all.

3. **Internal Conflict:** Hopefully by now you are realizing that internal conflict is inevitable, even among the best and loving of teams. How the conflict is dealt with makes all the difference. Not everyone can or should always get their way, including you as the team leader. Graciously dealing with internal conflict communicates this is a safe place to disagree, so we can publically be united.

4. **Team Disappointment:** Failure is never Final! Feel the loss, disappointment, or pain of what your team has faced. Help define in words its meaning. Use it as motivation, a chance to restructure, learn, work harder/smarter, and cast vision for a better tomorrow. Denial is never a productive strategy to dealing with disappointment.

5. **Team Success:** Be sure to celebrate wins, big and small, along the way. Wins in the church context could range from a record breaking attendance Sunday, another small group added, a Core Value being demonstrated, or a soul being saved. Be specific about different teammates' roles in this success. Call them out by name. Thank them in front of their peers. Write a thank you note for a job well done. Always be on the lookout for wins/successes to celebrate.

What opportunities do we currently have as a team to draw closer and stronger?

_____

_____

Of the 5 opportunities for a team to develop loving acceptance, which one should you focus on first? How might you turn what appears to be a negative into a positive?

_____

_____

Each of these lessons I've learned along my life-time were not taught in Bible School, but have been critical to the Lord using me and making an impact in the lives of others, and in the teams I have had the privilege to lead. These lessons are learned by some, missed by others. None the less, they are critical to making a significant difference.

If you miss these, you miss your potential. In order to harness the power of teamwork, the conclusion I've discovered is *"WE'RE BETTER TOGETHER"*.

Let me share with you the words of Solomon from Proverbs 1, as wisdom shouts from the streets:

20 Out in the open wisdom calls aloud,
she raises her voice in the public square;
21 on top of the wall she cries out,
at the city gate she makes her speech:
22 "How long will you who are simple love your simple
ways?
How long will mockers delight in mockery
and fools hate knowledge?
23 Repent at my rebuke!
Then I will pour out my thoughts to you,
I will make known to you my teachings.
24 But since you refuse to listen when I call
and no one pays attention when I stretch out my hand,
25 since you disregard all my advice
and do not accept my rebuke,

²⁶ I in turn will laugh when disaster strikes you;
  I will mock when calamity overtakes you—
²⁷ when calamity overtakes you like a storm,
  when disaster sweeps over you like a whirlwind,
    when distress and trouble overwhelm you.
²⁸ "Then they will call to me but I will not answer;
    they will look for me but will not find me,
      ²⁹ since they hated knowledge
      and did not choose to fear the LORD.
³⁰ Since they would not accept my advice
        and spurned my rebuke,
      ³¹ they will eat the fruit of their ways
    and be filled with the fruit of their schemes.
³² For the waywardness of the simple will kill them,
  and the complacency of fools will destroy them;
    ³³ but whoever listens to me will live in safety
    and be at ease, without fear of harm."

Chapter 10

THE TRUST EQUATION

Even so the body is not made up
of one part but of many.
(1 Corinthians 12:14)

A family of origin provides an immense foundation for how one perceives their relationship with God. For example, a young man whose father was an alcoholic and came home drunk and abusive of a boy's mother may have a difficult time viewing God as a loving Heavenly Father. Most people will make an effort to present themselves publicly as confident and cordial, but when situations become personal and they get close relationally, the darker side of the personal makeup may come through. Many adults struggle with childhood perceptions that were developed in the family. These early years of being taught distrust can be overcome through a renewal of the mind as the biblical model of God as our Father replaces the images of our youth. But, learning to trust others in difficult situations can be very challenging.

Personally, I had the advantage of being raised in a home that was healthy both spiritually and emotionally. I learned early in life that my father and mother were reliable. I could trust their word. If they promised they would do something, it was rare that they did not follow up and do what they said. If they could not fulfill their promise, there was a good reason.

As years went by in ministry, it wasn't long before people in the church, and sometimes even other ministers, would let me down. As a boy I learned to trust my parents; which made it easier to trust God as well as others around me. However, it didn't take long before I learned that not everyone is trustworthy. For instance, one friend that I trusted was discovered to be having an affair with a lady in his church. This pastor was a good guy who found himself ensnared by his own emotions during a vulnerable time in his life. These revelations of moral failure are not common, but when they occur it can shake you up, realizing that these failures can happen to anyone if we don't keep ourselves daily in a place of accountability and close relationship to the Lord and our spouse.

Initially this may not seem relevant when addressing the qualities of a team. However, there is no more important team setting than the team you and I call our family. If a husband is not faithful to his wife, how can the ministry team he is on trust him to be loyal to them?

The simple point is that trust is earned through a consistency in life over a period of time. A leader cannot demand trust from those who are on the team. Trust is earned from the character that is displayed by a leader who is committed to the team and committed to the purposes of the team, especially during difficult or challenging times.

In team leadership, there are often two competing principles that come into play. The first is that the team must be committed to something bigger than themselves. The task or goal is what becomes the glue that gives direction and purpose for the team. At the same time, the people who make up the team are critically important. There are times when individuals take priority over the purpose of the team and there are times when the task must take priority over the issues of the individuals. This is a difficult balance that every leader faces. When a team member is not able to function to the level required for the team's effectiveness to be maintained, then a decision must be made as to whether to keep the member or to excuse that individual for the benefit of the team.

In professional sports, the success of the team overrides the value of the individual. When the individual ceases to add the expected qualities (points, touchdowns, etc...), they are released and the team moves on from there. That is also true many times in the corporate world. As has been said, "It's not personal, only business." In the church, our values are different. This greatly complicates the decision for the leader. The task drives our purpose but the individual is valued as a member of the Body of Christ, not just a piece of machinery that can be discarded when broken. Redemption is a key value that permeates the Gospel message and activity.

This changes the way we do things in the church and creates a tension unlike most other team dynamics. For the leader to be trusted, processing this with the team is critical so everyone is aware of the boundaries and limitation to continuing on the team. While pastoring, a situation developed where I had to decide between two individuals who were committed to certain actions that were diametrically opposed. They were incompatible so I had to make the call. I was faced with the dilemma of choosing between persons. Would my choice be based on relationships or principles? It was not easy, but the result created a great bond in the team and a great trust in me as their leader. The pain of losing the other individual was hurtful, but the trust that was the result proved the decision was the best in what was a no win situation.

Accurately deciphering the difference is critical. On the one hand, if the individuals take precedence over the task, nothing will ever be accomplished. On the other hand, if the task is always the priority, then people can be used and abused for the sake of the task. Neither approach is always appropriate. There will never be a list of situations that can be consulted to make the determination on which way to go on this issue, but making the right call will influence the team member's level of trust in their leader.

The following insights are taken from my son's blog (www.JasonTourville.com) and may provide some helpful guidance when establishing trust. The blog's title is WHEN RELATIONSHIP AND LEADERSHIP COLLIDE:

For anyone who has been in leadership any amount of time, you have discovered the periodic collision between Relationship and Leadership. It could be a loving parent who now has to "lead" their child into obedience when they don't want to follow, screaming "I hate you" as they slam the door to their bedroom. Perhaps it is the one who receives an inner office promotion and now has to lead, direct, and even sometimes correct those with whom they had previously been peers. Then again, maybe you're the new kid on the block, trying to build relationships of trust with your team, yet at the same time difficult decisions need to be made to assure the success of the organization, team, ministry, etc... It is in these moments where 2-worlds collide.

So what does a leader do and how do they decide when there is apparent collision between your leadership (and the realistic expectations of your role) and the relationships you've been entrusted to manage and lead? After 22 years of ministry and leadership I certainly don't have this perfectly mastered, but below are a few insights I've gained along the way:

1. **Always VALUE the Person**: There are ways to value the person, while not allowing the relationship to be leveraged (or manipulated). Remember, if you value the relationship over your leadership, you will most likely lose both. Besides, if the person you are leading values the relationship, they will respect your leadership. When you as the leader value the person, you build trust with the other team members, even when the difficult leadership decisions collide with the relationship.

2. **Understand Leadership Timing**: Forward movement always takes concerted and focused energy. A wise leader understands when to push forward toward progress, and when it is a suicide mission. If you are the "new kid" you will certainly want to tread slowly, unless you are borrowing leadership strength and backing from a superior.

3. **Lead for the Long-Haul**: With the risk of using aggressive language, you can win the battle, but lose the war. As leaders we cannot become so fixate on one instance or conflict that we forget how this plays into the bigger

picture of what we are called to do, and who we need to be. I believe this was the context of Proverbs 19:11, "*A person's wisdom yields patience; it is to one's glory to overlook an offense.*" As God for the wisdom of when to "overlook."

4. **Recognize the 2-Faces of Peace**: I have noticed there are Peace-Makers and there are Peace-Keepers. In <u>Matthew 5:9</u>, Jesus said, "*Blessed are the peacemakers, for they will be called children of God.*" A true Peace-Maker cares enough to confront. A Peace-Keeper on the other hand will sweep conflict under the rug, appease the contemptuous party, and placate the critical. While in the moment you may gain peace, Peace-Keeping leadership always breeds distrust and diseased culture. Peace-Makers will confront with love and with the hope of restoration and unity. Unity is the result of right relationship with humble leadership.

5. **Never Walk Alone**: While leadership may be lonely, leadership should never be "done alone." Healthy leadership has the context of healthy relationships. The final thought about leadership and relationships is to make sure you are proactive in building healthy relationships with your team. When challenging times come (and they will), your team or its member will know that you care even if they disagree. This doesn't mean that your leadership will never be challenged or your decisions or character questioned, but

you'll have a relational record that speaks for itself. Proverbs 20:11 puts it this way, *"Even small children are known by their actions, so is their conduct really pure and upright?"* Invest in relationships before the collision.

One final thought, Always Stay Ahead of the Wave. My boys and I love to boogie board surf when we're at the shore (that's the Ocean for all you non-East-coasters). If you're behind the wave, you've missed your chance to "surf" and in some ways abdicate a portion of your leadership. If you meet the wave as it is crashing, you may be crushed by the fury of the wave. The astute boogie boarder (and leader) has their eyes scanning the waters, determining when to move and on which waves to surf. If you don't stay ahead of the wave, the wave will get ahead of you. Leadership and relationships are not an either/or but a both/and dynamic. Trust is built when strong leadership and strong relationships co-exist!

When discussing the growth of our district, one of our national leaders asked me, "What are you doing to see this happen, or did you just win the lottery?" (In all honesty, I wasn't sure whether to take the question as an insult or a compliment.) The reason for the question is that the PennDel Ministry Network has gone from about 360 church to over 430 churches in the last ten years. We have received the national award for church planting for the last few years in a row. Did we win the lottery? No way! What has happen is not a chance development. We have worked hard to develop a healthy culture of reproduction, relationship and resourcing the ministers of our network, not just the setting of goals and expecting short term successes.

We have intentionally endeavored to build a climate of trust with our people so that what is important to them for kingdom building will be important to us. The Presbytery has been amazingly supportive in breaking down territorialism, investing funds to plant churches, revitalize existing churches, and helping scholarship our ministers toward life-long learning and growth. They have released our staff to flourish in their callings and build ministries that effectively reach the lost and equip believers to be all God has called them to be. Our departmental leaders along with their support personnel, continuously effectively impact the various segments of the population in Pennsylvania and Delaware. It is all about the team of leaders God has raised up in our network.

In his book, *The Speed of Trust*, Stephen Covey has captured a secret that can be easily missed. When a leader trusts the team and each team member trusts the leader as well as the other members of the team, the effects of the unity, that is the result, produces incredible change and lasting transformation. When trust is missing, the potential for misunderstanding, division, party spirits, and lack of unity to name a few, is great. When trust exists, the team will be able to accomplish almost anything.

Someone has said, "It is amazing what can be accomplished if we don't care who gets the credit." Better Together summarizes the dynamic required in harnessing the power of team work. For those of us in the PennDel Ministry Network the credit goes to the many individuals who have embraced their roll within the team we call the church of Jesus Christ. No one gets all the credit but the glory goes to Jesus. I have often said that the task of the ministry is largely to stay out of God's way so He can do what he wants to do.

When individuals are committed to follow the Lord's leading in their lives and ministries, the whole of the Church will effectively move forward and reach lost people for Christ.

1. **Take a moment to describe the dynamics of trust in all directions (between you and your team, your team toward you, and your team members toward each other):**

   _____

   _____

   _____

2. **What gaps might there be when it comes to issues of trust?**

   _____

   _____

   _____

3. **What might build a great culture of trust within your team and organization?**

   _____

   _____

   _____

OUR DREAM TEAM:

Those of us at the PennDel Ministry Center play a role of administrating the overall system of the district. Don Immel, along with Dave Crosby before him, manage the details of administrative issues in the Secretary-Treasurer's office with precision and excellence. Tom Rees is an incredible connector of people and resources. I have often referred to him as my right hand man. He understands the way I think and has the ability to articulate my vision with clarity and passion. Doug Sayers has led the Youth Department for over twenty-five years, continually making changes to stay relevant with the students across our network while stressing the fundamentals of the Spirit-anointed and spirit-led discipleship for our youth. George Krebs leads our discipleship efforts, children's ministries and the Bongiorno Conference Center with the personal touch that empowers others to be their best for Christ. Arnold Wheatley works behind the scenes with our technology to provide the infrastructure electronically to enable us to stay current in a rapidly changing digital age. Then, what can I say about Carole Bongiorno who has taken our graphic design, both print and web presence, to an entirely different level. Greg Scott leads the boys of our Royal Rangers, training and mentoring them to become men of God for the future. Sharon Poole leads our Girls Ministry to equip and encourage the young ladies of our fellowship. Ruth Puleo leads our Women of Purpose with incredible skill, effectiveness and excellence. The other individual staff support personnel work hard to serve our network and their efforts are invaluable. Steve Provard, Sue Stumpo, Penny Wheatley, Megan Jordan, Robin Immel, Mark Gettis, Jessica Jones, Christa Fowler, Lee Rogers, Linda Reynolds, Lynette Provard, and Rhonda Imes are some of the unsung heroes that make us who we are.

As wonderful as all these individual team members are to me personally as well as to the district, none of us can make the district grow. It is the pastors and leaders of our network who are the heroes of the story of *Better Together*. There are so many people who have made a difference in our journey as lead by our district Presbytery. Part of our system is what we call the C3 Leadership Network. Bryan Koch facilitates the Catalyst Groups who champion the church planting initiatives of our district. Jeff Leake who discovered years ago that if he worked more on the concern God has (lost people and the need for more life giving churches) then God would take care of his problem (inadequate parking for his church) has responded to God's vision to Reach Northeast through church planting, not only in PennDel but throughout the Northeast of the United States. Brian Bolt began to connect with Jeff and now leads the CityReach Network which now has scores of churches that are reaching lost people. Gerry Stoltzfoos has been a mentor, friend and encourager to many who are planting churches and reaching the unsaved. Steve DeFrain has a vision to reach the younger generations by planting churches that he and his son are establishing. The immigrants who are coming to our nation, and specifically to Pennsylvania and Delaware, need pastors and churches to partner with them to establish churches that can minister to those coming to our areas. David Twiss, Kurt Jenkins, Jeff Marshall, Tim Halbfoerster, Jim Balzano, Bob Novak, Phil Menditto, Roland Coon and Chad Stoecker are among the many who not only understand the importance of building their own congregation, but are also initiating satellite churches that will reach beyond the walls of their own buildings and establish points of contact for many others who will come to faith in Christ.

Quite frankly, no one has the ability to build the kingdom. Jesus said he would build his church. Our role is to cooperate with what he wants to do. The #1 Cultural value and activity for every team, I believe, is trust. This is the one quality that is indispensable for us in the Body of Christ. The Psalmist (133) expressed it so well, "How good and pleasant it is when brothers dwell together in unity" (vs.1) "for there the Lord bestows his blessing, even life for evermore" (vs.3). Where there is trust there can be unity, and that is where you will find God's favor, blessing and anointing of His Holy Spirit.

ADDITIONAL RESOURCES

CHURCH MINISTRIES

- **Antagonist in the Church** by Kenneth C. Haugk
- **Leading Turnaround Churches** by Gene Wood
- **Cracking Your Churche's Culture Code** by Samuel R. Chand

EMOTIONAL INTELLIGENCE

- **Primal Leadership** by Daniel Goleman, Annie McKee, and Richard E. Boyatzis
- **The Emotional Intelligence Quick Book** by Travis Bradberry and Jean Greaves
- **Managing Yourself** by Harvard Business Review

LEADERSHIP DEVELOPMENT

- **The 3 Keys to Empowerment** by Ken Blanchard, John P. Carlos, and Alan Randolph
- **Leading Change** by John P. Kotter

SPIRITUAL DEVELOPMENT

- **How People Grow** by Henry Cloud and John Townsend
- **Living in the Spirit** by George O. Wood

TEAM LEADERSHIP

- **Bench Strength** by Robert Barner, Ph.D.
- **Encouraging the Heart** by James M. Kouzes and Barry Z. Posner
- **Leading So Others Can Follow** by James T. Bradford

ABOUT THE AUTHORS

DR. STEPHEN R. TOURVILLE

Stephen R. Tourville is currently Superintendent of the PennDel Ministry Network of the Assemblies of God. Prior to that he was Intercultural Ministries Director with the Assemblies of God, PennDel District Home Missions Director, and pastored in Pennsylvania for 25 years.

Stephen has a Doctor of Ministry and Master of Arts degree from the Assemblies of God Theological Seminary (now Evangel University) His doctoral project was entitled, *"Training Pastors in Emotional Intelligence and Situational Leadership Skills.* His Master of Divinity is from Evangelical School of Theology, and his B.S. in Bible and Theology from the University of Valley Forge. He was the recipient of the Allen J. Bodey Award in Expository Preaching while earning his Master of Divinity and the 2013 Alumnus of the Year at the AG Theological Seminary.

He and Marjie have conducted marriage seminars, spoken at local church functions within the PennDel District, and participated in international ministry on five continents. His hobbies include reading, music (guitar, trombone, singing) and astronomy. They have two children and six grandchildren.

He is passionate about empowering individuals to fulfill their calling in serving God through Pentecostal ministry.

JASON A. TOURVILLE

Jason Tourville is a husband, father, pastor, athlete, and author. He currently leads a thriving church, Shrewsbury Assembly, since January 2013, and has been a full-time minister with the Assemblies of God since graduation from the University of Valley Forge in 1995, where he was a 1st-Team All-American basketball player.

After ministering as a Youth Pastor in Delaware, he continued his education at Assemblies of God Theological Seminary, a MA in Counseling (MFT, LPC). He has served at a variety of churches in the Northeast, from mega-churches, to small start-up churches.

He has launched a compassion outreach in Philadelphia in 2010, founded of www.BreakthroughPastors.com, an online ministry encouraging and inspiring pastors in the *Spiritual Dynamic of Leadership,* and you can find his weekly thoughts at his personal blog www.JasonTourville.com.

He has also written Discipleship Training materials to equip followers of Christ to reach their full potential. The courses include: "Starting Line," "Training for the Prize," "Stepping on to the Field," and "Helping others Win." He enjoys reading, all sports and has participated in a few triathlons, including finishing an Ironman 70.3 and has climbed Mt. Kilimanjaro.

He now lives Southern York County, PA with his wife Rene' with their four kids (two boys and two girls) and a dog. What free-time is found, he likes spending with his family, and watching the kids in their interests.